The Historical Imagination of G.K. Chesterton

Studies in Major Literary Authors
WILLIAM E. CAIN, *General Editor*

For a full list of titles in this series, please visit www.routledge.com

Melville's Monumental Imagination
Ian S. Maloney

Writing "Out of All the Camps"
J.M. Coetzee's Narratives of Displacement
Laura Wright

Here and Now
The Politics of Social Space in D. H. Lawrence and Virginia Woolf
Youngjoo Son

"Unnoticed in the Casual Light of Day"
Philip Larkin and the Plain Style
Tijana Stojković

Queer Times
Christopher Isherwood's Modernity
Jamie M. Carr

Edith Wharton's "Evolutionary Conception"
Darwinian Allegory in Her Major Novels
Paul J. Ohler

The End of Learning
Milton and Education
Thomas Festa

Reading and Mapping Hardy's Roads
Scott Rode

Creating Yoknapatawpha
Readers and Writers in Faulkner's Fiction
Owen Robinson

No Place for Home
Spatial Constraint and Character Flight in the Novels of Cormac McCarthy
Jay Ellis

The Machine that Sings
Modernism, Hart Crane, and the Culture of the Body
Gordon A. Tapper

Influential Ghosts
A Study of Auden's Sources
Rachel Wetzsteon

D.H. Lawrence's Border Crossing
Colonialism in His Travel Writings and "Leadership" Novels
Eunyoung Oh

Dorothy Wordsworth's Ecology
Kenneth R. Cervelli

Sports, Narrative, and Nation in the Fiction of F. Scott Fitzgerald
Jarom Lyle McDonald

Shelley's Intellectual System and its Epicurean Background
Michael A. Vicario

Modernist Aesthetics and Consumer Culture in the Writings of Oscar Wilde
Paul L. Fortunato

Milton's Uncertain Eden
Understanding Place in *Paradise Lost*
Andrew Mattison

Henry Miller and Religion
Thomas Nesbit

The Magic Lantern
Representation of the Double in Dickens
Maria Cristina Paganoni

The Environmental Unconscious in the Fiction of Don DeLillo
Elise A. Martucci

James Merrill
Knowing Innocence
Reena Sastri

Yeats and Theosophy
Ken Monteith

Pynchon and the Political
Samuel Thomas

Paul Auster's Postmodernity
Brendan Martin

Editing Emily Dickinson
The Production of an Author
Lena Christensen

Cormac McCarthy and the Myth of American Exceptionalism
John Cant

Our Scene is London
Ben Jonson's City and the Space of the Author
James D. Mardock

Poetic Language and Political Engagement in the Poetry of Keats
Jack Siler

Politics and Aesthetics in *The Diary of Virginia Woolf*
Joanne Campbell Tidwell

Homosexuality in the Life and Work of Joseph Conrad
Love Between the Lines
Richard J. Ruppel

Shakespeare in the Victorian Periodicals
Kathryn Prince

Shakespeare and the Economic Imperative
"What's aught but as 'tis valued?"
Peter F. Grav

Wallace Stevens and the Realities of Poetic Language
Stefan Holander

Milton and the Spiritual Reader
Reading and Religion in Seventeenth-Century England
David Ainsworth

Everybody's America
Thomas Pynchon, Race, and the Cultures of Postmodernism
David Witzling

Dickens, Journalism, and Nationhood
Mapping the World in Household Words
Sabine Clemm

Narrative Conventions and Race in the Novels of Toni Morrison
Jennifer Lee Jordan Heinert

Philip K. Dick
Canonical Writer of the Digital Age
Lejla Kucukalic

The Historical Imagination of G.K. Chesterton
Locality, Patriotism, and Nationalism
Joseph R. McCleary

The Historical Imagination of G.K. Chesterton

Locality, Patriotism, and Nationalism

Joseph R. McCleary

First published 2009
by Routledge
270 Madison Ave, New York, NY 10016

Simultaneously published in the UK
by Routledge
2 Park Square, Milton Park, Abingdon, Oxon OX14 4RN

Routledge is an imprint of the Taylor & Francis Group, an informa business

© 2009 Taylor & Francis

Typeset in Sabon by IBT Global.
Printed and bound in the United States of America on acid-free paper by IBT Global.

All rights reserved. No part of this book may be reprinted or reproduced or utilised in any form or by any electronic, mechanical, or other means, now known or hereafter invented, including photocopying and recording, or in any information storage or retrieval system, without permission in writing from the publishers.

Trademark Notice: Product or corporate names may be trademarks or registered trademarks, and are used only for identification and explanation without intent to infringe. Every effort has been made to contact copyright holders for their permission to reprint material in this book. The publishers would be grateful to hear from any copyright holder who is not here acknowledged and will undertake to rectify any errors or omissions in future editions of this book.

Library of Congress Cataloging in Publication Data
McCleary, Joseph R.
  The historical imagination of G.K. Chesterton : locality, patriotism, and nationalism / Joseph R. McCleary.
    p. cm.—(Studies in major literary authors)
  Includes bibliographical references and index.
  1. Chesterton, G. K. (Gilbert Keith), 1874–1936—Criticism and interpretation.
  2. Chesterton, G. K. (Gilbert Keith), 1874–1936—Philosophy. 3. Chesterton, G. K. (Gilbert Keith), 1874–1936—Knowledge—History. 4. History—Philosophy.
  5. Patriotism in literature. 6. Nationalism in literature. I. Title.
  PR4453.C4Z723 2009
  828'.912—dc22
                          2008037997

ISBN10: 0-415-99175-7 (hbk)
ISBN10: 0-203-88225-3 (ebk)

ISBN13: 978-0-415-99175-9 (hbk)
ISBN13: 978-0-203-88225-2 (ebk)

G.K. Chesterton 1904. Alan Langdon Coburn.

For Mary

Contents

Acknowledgments		xiii
Introduction		1
1	The Critics and Chesterton's Philosophy of History	7
2	Influences and Contemporaries	34
3	The Critical Lens	57
4	The Creative Lens	83
5	The Critical and Creative Legacy: Dawson, Waugh, and McLuhan	116
6	Conclusion: Locality, Patriotism, and Nationalism and One Lens More	132
Notes		141
Bibliography		151
Index		157

Acknowledgements

I would like to acknowledge the inspiration and encouragement of my many teachers. Prominent among these are Robert Jackson, Virgil Nemoianu, and Joseph Sendry.

I would also like to thank my children, Jacqueline, Alexandra, and Teddy, for their love and patience.

The help of my wife, Mary, was indispensable. And her love remains so.

Introduction

Gilbert Keith Chesterton was born in Kensington, England on May 29, 1874, to Edward and Marie Chesterton. He was the middle child of three, and his upbringing was that of comfortable middle-class family. Chesterton was educated at St. Paul's School in London and later studied art at The Slade School. He married Frances Blogg on June 28, 1901, and the marriage was a happy one. His writing career began during his schooldays and continued unabated throughout his life. The most striking feature of Chesterton's writing is its sheer volume and variety. Between the publication of his first book in 1900 and his death on June 14, 1936, he produced one hundred books and innumerable articles.[1] The most important influence on Chesterton's intellectual life was his search for a creed to give coherence to his life. He found it in the Catholic Church and, after his conversion in 1922, became an apologist for his new faith. His writing comprises history, poetry, novels, literary criticism, biography, essays, detective stories, plays, and short stories. This book is primarily concerned with his philosophy of history as it is expressed through a selection of his critical and creative work.

The interlocking themes of locality, patriotism, and nationalism constituted the essential elements of the philosophy of history that informed much of G.K. Chesterton's critical and literary work. Patriotism and nationalism can be distinguished as twin outgrowths of locality. Locality is a general term encompassing the customs, language, terrain, and religious beliefs of a people who share some meaningful contact because they live in proximity to each other. While patriotism looks inward and is characterized by protective impulses and improvement, nationalism is outwardly directed and driven by aggressive impulses, with a spirit of subjugation in its more extreme forms. Chesterton emphasized the strategic role localism has played in societies from every era. He took particular interest in studying the historical interplay of patriotism, nationalism, and localism during the medieval period of English history. His historical observations of this period, as with other periods, were strongly influenced by his Catholic beliefs and his role as a Catholic apologist. The relation between his interest in locality and his Catholic faith can be seen in the following passage from *A Short History of England:*

> At the beginning of the Dark Ages the great pagan cosmopolitan society now grown Christian was as much a slave state as old South Carolina. By the fourteenth century it was almost as much a state of peasant proprietors as modern France. No laws had been passed against slavery; no dogmas even had condemned it by definition; no war had been waged against it, no new race or ruling caste had repudiated it; but it was gone. This startling and silent transformation is perhaps the best measure of the pressure of popular life in the Middle Ages, of how fast it was making new things in its spiritual factory. Like everything else in the medieval revolution, from its cathedrals to its ballads, it was as anonymous as it was enormous. It is admitted that the conscious and active emancipators everywhere were the parish priests and the religious brotherhoods.[2]

The emphasis Chesterton places on the impact of local groupings—parishes and monasteries—is characteristic of an historical outlook that deems locality preferable to the state as a category of analysis.[3] A thorough inventory of Chesterton's philosophy of history as it is expressed through the themes of patriotism, nationalism, and locality must necessarily encompass his socio-political commentary on the late Victorian and Edwardian age in which the author lived. But true to his expansive view, Chesterton drew lessons from history by studying different eras. While Chesterton expounded upon the lessons of history in his properly historical works, such as *The Everlasting Man,* he employed the full force of his creative talent to apply these lessons through imagery and paradox in his literary output. Chesterton was an artist with a strong visual sense coupled with a keen perception of the similarities and differences of things. His mode of thought was highly dependent on imagination and intuition. These abilities were shown in his poems, stories, and novels, where he attempted to reconcile the bewildering variety of life and the natural human effort to find coherence.

There was a sharp contrast between the public and oral aspects of Chesterton's poetry and the more private aspect of his novels. In both forms, however, one sees the treatment of the same intertwining themes of locality, patriotism and nationalism. Chesterton's philosophy of history is particularly evident in the novels: *The Ball and the Cross, The Napoleon of Notting Hill,* and *The Man Who Was Thursday.* Similarly, he explores historical themes in the poetical works, *The Ballad of the White Horse* and *Lepanto.* He highlights the sense of the unexpected and paradox in all of these works to demonstrate his philosophical views.

Critics trying to make sense of Chesterton's emphasis on unpredictability sometimes fail to trace it back to the roots of his view on the nature of things. Hence the need for research to explore the connections between

Chesterton's evident philosophical powers and his intense imaginative appreciation of particulars, especially those particulars that make up history and are manifest in the critical and creative body of his work. I contend that his powerful imagination served to enhance his intellectual grasp of specific contours of English history and put a distinctive stamp on his philosophical thought. This capacity was identified by historians and critics alike, such as Raymond Las Vergnas who noted that:

> The paradoxical quality ... explains to no small degree the position that Chesterton occupies and will always retain in English literature. Our author is appreciated, in England, not only for the profundity and nobility of his ideal, but quite as much—perhaps more—for his transcendent absurdities. A spring-tide shone in his eyes, because his eyes were children's eyes, always on the look-out for the unexpected. The English are grateful to him for it. The author ... has become one of England's greatest writers, by reason of the effortless genius of his childishnesses. [4]

The imagination of childhood is generally understood to be vivid and supple, two qualities that characterize Chesterton's adult writing.

But if his imagination retained a childlike quality, his movement from a vague agnosticism to Catholic apologist called for an adult appraisal of the environment in which he wrote. He was not unaware of the potential ramifications in his defending and pursuing a stand that might be at odds with prevalent currents. This was certainly the case with his decision to convert to Catholicism in a country where the Roman Church was often viewed with disdain. Chesterton's commitment to remain constant in his pursuit of truth led even those who passionately disagreed with him, such as his friend George Bernard Shaw, to esteem him highly. One can identify how the idealism of the youth met with the wisdom of the elder in his own assessment of the cost-benefit relation of such dogged espousal of principle:

> People who say that an ideal is a dangerous thing, that it deludes and intoxicates, are perfectly right. But the ideal which intoxicates most is the least idealistic kind of ideal. The ideal which intoxicates least is the very ideal ideal; that sobers us suddenly, as all heights and precipices and great distances do. [5]

This sense of the seriousness of his Catholicism was combined with a sense of humor that finds a place in his historical thought. His openness to paradox and the unexpected is related to humor because both humor and this openness require a sensitivity to incongruity. While this book focuses on the theme of locality in relation to a philosophy of history, I will also point out the way that humor necessarily has a part in a philosophy of history that finds coherence in locality.

Chesterton's views on patriotism and nationalism, with their common grounding in the particular traits of the local populace, were very much guided by his own subjective analysis. His critical style is broad and direct, as is evident in the following passage from his book, *As I Was Saying*:

> I do not want the English or anybody else to be international in the sense of cosmopolitan. Christendom has developed in a national form; and men who have no patriotism are not inside Europe but rather outside it. A Frenchman who does not love France, an Englishman who does not love England, is a bad European and not a good European.[6]

This is typical of Chesterton's view that one need not be disloyal to one's own people in acknowledging the good things of larger groupings. As will be explained further in the following chapters, Chesterton advanced the theory that true progress in history could only be found in the unified principles of personal integrity and a commitment to advancing the noble aspirations of one's community and eventually one's country. This seemingly simplistic approach had the air of being old-fashioned even in Chesterton's day. It was based not on blind devotion, however, but rather on his appraisal of the respective strengths and weaknesses of his nation with a view to upholding the former and amending the latter.

Chesterton's philosophy of history thus had roots in both his personal ideals and in his understanding of human nature and the local origins of all historical movement. This confluence of Chesterton the private thinker and the critical, creative historical observer was to mark his writings with a substantial coherence that resulted from an openness to unexpected conclusions. He would accept and incorporate into his thought whatever his observations revealed. We can preview his thinking on the subject in the chapter "Paying for Patriotism" from *The Common Man*:

> As a matter of fact, I am one of the few people left, of my own sort and calling, who do still believe in patriotism; just as I am among the few who do still believe in democracy. Both these ideas were exaggerated extravagantly and, what is worse, erroneously, or entirely in the wrong way, during the nineteenth century; but the reaction against them today is very strong, especially among the intellectuals. But I do believe that patriotism rests on a psychological truth; a social sympathy with those of our own sort, whereby we see our own potential acts in them; and understand their history from within. . . . But if we accept this mystical corporate being, this larger self, we must accept it for good and ill. If we boast of our best, we must repent of our worst. Otherwise patriotism will be a very poor thing indeed.[7]

Here Chesterton shows an inclination to conform to an external reality combined with a recognition that human nature helps explain the actions of others. This inclination is consistent with his role as Catholic apologist because of the Thomistic realist philosophy whose pride of place in Catholicism Chesterton recognized in his own writings.[8] What makes Chesterton's philosophy of history distinctive is his Catholic worldview combined with a highly imaginative emphasis on locality and the sub-themes that locality entails. In this book I will examine these sub-themes, principally patriotism and nationalism, as they are expressed and elaborated in his critical and creative work. Further, I will contend that locality, which engenders reactions of patriotism or nationalism on the level of human action, is also connected significantly to the concepts of creaturehood, specificity and free will in Chesterton's philosophy of history.

This book is divided into five main chapters. I will use an analytical close reading together with an approach that takes into account the interface of the philosophical, religious, and aesthetic, ultimately placing Chesterton's work inside the historical context (nineteenth and twentieth century) in which it was created.

Chapter one will deal with the criticism of Chesterton's work that focuses on his philosophy of history as it is expressed in the themes of locality, patriotism, and nationalism. I will examine the works of the major biographers (Pearce, Dale, Ffinch, Barker, Titterton, Coren, Ward) and critics (Kenner, Lauer, Wills, Hollis, Corrin). I will note the similarities and differences among various critics. I also refer to the ideas of Hobsbawm, Gellner, and Millon-Delsol to provide a point of reference from figures in the historical profession as opposed to the literary.

The second chapter will outline the philosophies of history espoused by some of Chesterton's literary predecessors and contemporaries. Bloom's critical approach will open the discussion, followed by an analysis of the influence of Hilaire Belloc and H.G. Wells. Both Belloc and Wells were contemporary influences on Chesterton. However, the effect of Belloc on Chesterton was derived from their personal friendship, whereas that of Wells was more the result of their rivalry. The discussion will continue with Chesterton's assessment of another figure of substantial impact, George Bernard Shaw. Two major predecessors of Chesterton, William Cobbett and Sir Walter Scott, will be studied for their considerable influence on him. The chapter puts these influences in the context of nineteenth century historical writing with an examination of the historians Buckle, Lecky, Green, Froude, and Acton.

Chapter three will explore how Chesterton's philosophy of history, articulated in the categories of localism, patriotism, and nationalism, impacts his literary criticism. *The Victorian Age in Literature* will be analyzed as well as Chesterton's critical studies on Dickens. These, together with his critiques of Chaucer, will be examined for the way in which they display Chesterton's historical categories at work on two widely separated eras of English literature.

Chapter four focuses on Chesterton's creative writing as it expresses his philosophy of history. *The Ball and the Cross, The Napoleon of Notting*

Hill, and *The Man Who Was Thursday* will be analyzed as narratives which, to enlarge on Boyd's phrase, define not only "a political view which is characteristic of the entire body of his fiction"[9], but also define an *historical* view that is equally characteristic. The poetry (*The Ballad of the White Horse* and *Lepanto*) will be treated under the same categories of locality, patriotism, and nationalism. These categories will be further explored by comparing the public and oral aspect of the poetry with the private aspect of the novel form, highlighting the historical relationships derived from this contrast.

Finally, chapter five will provide a discussion of the general influence of Chesterton's specifically historical categories on three later writers with a Catholic orientation whose preoccupations mirror the three hinges on which this study turns: Christopher Dawson, a historian; Evelyn Waugh, a novelist; and Marshall McLuhan, a critic.

I will also offer a consideration of some modern approaches to historiography as it relates to literature and draw brief parallels with Chesterton's views. I will then sum up Chesterton's distinctive use of locality, with its outgrowths of nationalism and patriotism, as an idea that unifies history and gives it coherence. This unifying idea provides a framework for understanding: a philosophy. I will show this philosophy to be expounded through critical works and creative works because one is a tool best suited to examining a reality already given and the other produces new realities to persuade and teach. Both kinds of work will be shown to be lenses through which Chesterton's philosophy of history is made clear. Furthermore, I will point out the way in which Chesterton's emphasis on locality blends the concepts of free will, specificity, and creaturehood. Having shown the importance of the critical and creative exposition of locality, I will conclude with a consideration of humor as a third lens that allows one to look on Chesterton's philosophy of history from the broadest perspective of the three.

1 The Critics and Chesterton's Philosophy of History

G.K. Chesterton's approach to the study to history was informed to a large extent by his view that individuals rather than larger systems, ideologies, institutions or governments, are the primary forces of historical movement. One prominent modern historian, Eric Hobsbawm, has spoken about the various approaches to the writing of history, pointing out that one must make a selection:

> All historical study therefore implies making a selection, a tiny selection of some things out of the infinity of human activities in the past, and of what affected those activities. But there is no generally accepted criterion for making such a selection, and to the extent that there is one at any given time, it is likely to change. When historians thought history was largely determined by great men, their selection was obviously different from what it is when they don't.[1]

Though perhaps insufficient, the "great man" theory of history points to Chesterton's understanding that while history may not be solely the product of great men, it is nevertheless the product of individuals who come from specific locations and have distinctive stories, languages, and surroundings, and who are motivated by the customs, history and culture of their respective localities.

Chesterton called for a new approach to the study of history that would take into account the determining factor of the individual and specific localities. Chesterton described this "new history" as essentially psychological. He meant the word psychological in the etymological sense, namely, the history of a person's soul, with its ignorance and its knowledge, all of which was formed by where and with whom he or she had grown up. Climate, terrain, language, religion, family, and friends all combine to shape a person's soul. They also determine the movements of small groups of humanity that, taken in the aggregate form, determine the movements of history.

One of the most striking descriptions of historical causality to be found in Chesterton's writings is the following excerpt from *The Everlasting*

Man. This work, published in 1925, sets out Chesterton's argument for the importance of Christianity within the broad context of human history.

> In nothing is this new history needed so much as in the psychology of war. Our history is stiff with official documents, public or private, which tell us nothing of the thing itself. . . . There is something we all know which can only be rendered, in an appropriate language, as realpolitik. As a matter of fact, it is an almost insanely un-realpolitik. It is always stubbornly and stupidly repeating that men fight for material ends, without reflecting for a moment that the material ends are hardly ever material to the men who fight. In any case no man will die for practical politics, just as no man will die for pay. Nero could not hire a hundred Christians to be eaten by lions at a shilling an hour; for men will not be martyred for money. But the vision called up by realpolitik, or realistic politics, is beyond example crazy and incredible. Does anybody in the world believe that a soldier says, 'My leg is nearly dropping off, but I shall go on till it drops; for after all I shall enjoy all the advantages of my government obtaining a warm-water port in Finland . . . Whatever starts wars, the thing that sustains wars is something in the soul; that is something akin to religion. It is what men feel about life and about death. A man near to death is dealing directly with an absolute; it is nonsense to say that he is concerned only with relative and remote complications that death in any case will end. If he is sustained by certain loyalties, they must be loyalties as simple as death. They are generally two ideas, which are only two sides of one idea. This first is the love of something said to be threatened, if it be only vaguely known as home; the second is dislike and defiance of some strange thing that threatens it. [2]

Chesterton clearly identifies that it is only the promotion and/or defense of personal loyalties and ideals that can truly impel people into action. Chesterton also believed that the presence of legend, literature, art and music in a culture can articulate the commonly-held beliefs of a people, and are important motivational forces. The myth of the *Ballad of the White Horse* (1911) is an example.

By contrast, Hobsbawm believes that there should neither be nations nor divisions of people based on passion, myth-legend, or nationalism. Hobsbawn's approach to history calls for the elimination of national and ethnic myths as a motivational drive:

> But the fact that a new generation has grown up which can stand back from the passions of the great traumatic and formative moments of the countries' history is a sign of hope for historians. However, we cannot wait for the generations to pass. We must resist the *formation* of national, ethnic and other myths, as they are being formed. It will not make us popular. Thomas Masaryk, founder of the Czechoslovak

Republic, was not popular when he entered politics as the man who proved, with regret but without hesitation, that the medieval manuscripts on which much of the Czech national myth was based were fakes. But it has to be done, and I hope those of you who are historians will do it. [3]

Chesterton's vision is in such great contrast with Hobsbawm's view precisely because he thinks that local myths and passions are the essential sources of the human movement in time that we call history. He does not see myths or legends that embody the local features of a community to be necessary obstacles to human development. These formative stories may not literally be true in every respect, but they are emblems of commonly-held experiences.

The use of imaginative emblems has been noted by Sylvere Monod as the distinctive quality of Chesterton's historical thought:

> "It is like saying," Chesterton writes again and again, when he is about to show, through analogy, the inadequacy of some statement with which he disagrees and which he wants to persuade his readers is dangerously wrong. He produces powerful imaginative interpretations of history, of prehistory, and of thought.[4]

Monod is not sympathetic to the rhetorical ploys that he sees Chesterton using to make his points but he nonetheless acknowledges the power of his imagination to illuminate historical events. The imagination works on what can be pictured and this means that Chesterton will favor the specific over the general. The specific qualities of local realities favor the imaginative approach that Monod cites as both the weakness and strength of Chesterton's historical writing: "In his view, man can only know small observable things, and vast abstractions and inferences must remain suspicious."[5]

The meaning of history for Chesterton is therefore closely tied to all that is local. (For the purposes of this book, I will refer to this idea as "localism".) The bridge between localism and the nation is that nations rise based on population, complexity, specialization, and organization. These categories comprise the distinction of functions that builds infrastructure. Also, sufficient leisure brought about by the organization of functions enables literary forms such as narrative in song to be created. This, together with other creative and artistic endeavors, captures the experiences and values of a people.

One historian, Ernest Gellner, who studied the origin of nations and nationalism, has said that:

> Nationalism has been defined, in effect, as the striving to make culture and polity congruent, to endow a culture with its own political roof, and not more than one roof at that. [6]

Later, Gellner distinguishes nationalist sentiment as "the feeling of anger aroused by the violation of the principle [of nationalism], or the feeling of satisfaction aroused by its fulfillment."[7] Chesterton's emphasis on locality has similarities with Gellner's analysis in ascribing importance to cultural, and hence locally generated, forces as the foundation of any nationalism. Gellner's inclusion of anger as a passion connected with nationalism points to the possibility of aggressive impulses that I would distinguish from the ameliorative impulses of patriotism. As nationalism develops, it can move toward aggressive stands and lead to imperialism if the character of the people it represents tends toward aggression. The nuances of nationalism reflect the values of its people.

By contrast, patriotism is the natural, inwardly-focused love for the locally-inspired culture of a nation. The importance of land and geography is paramount to the formation of an early association and appreciation of local beauty, and the ensuing building of a familiarity with it. The English patriot may love the meadows of Sussex because they were part of his or her childhood years. However, this person would not despise the arid plains of Spain because he or she did not grow up there. Furthermore, patriotism recognizes the inherent quality of one's predecessors as those who were foundational forces in the building and development of the land.

Nationalism is the unifying of all the localities within certain boundaries that takes place when enough common ground—literally and figuratively—is established among people. Gellner emphasizes this unifying aspect of the political in relation to the cultural. He stresses the importance of the unity of education, and also the notion that cultural homogeneity is the product of the passage of time and a shared history.[8]

The sharing of language, customs, and beliefs that takes place on a local level may lead eventually to a political unity. Similarly, what takes place on the local and national levels corresponds to the family model in the complementarity and diversity of roles, resulting in the building of a single unit. Therefore, nationalism becomes not only the sum of its parts, but in so doing becomes a separate entity. Nationalism is informed by and, in turn, inspires its people.

There is a legitimate pride within patriotism for the customs, outlook and way of life of one's people. What ensues then is a natural desire to defend what is distinctive in a locality: its customs, language, values, and history. In his book, *The New Jerusalem*, published in 1920, Chesterton warns that patriotism must guard itself against a false glorification of the individual at the expense of the positive ideal of the nation as a whole:

> It is the vice of any patriotism or religion depending on race that the individual is himself the thing to be worshipped; the individual is his own ideal, and even his own idol. This fancy was fatal to the Germans; it is fatal to the Anglo-Saxons, whenever any of them forswear the

glorious name of Englishmen and Americans to fall into that forlorn description. This is not so when the nation is felt as a noble abstraction, of which the individual is proud in the abstract. A Frenchman is proud of France, and therefore may think himself unworthy of France. [9]

In *The Appetite of Tyranny* Chesterton goes further to describe the eventual imperialistic outcome when this tendency is carried to its extreme. He cites the manifestation of such imperialism in Germany in his characteristic mistrust of this tendency among its people:

'I am a German and you are a Chinaman. Therefore I, being a German, have a right to be a Chinaman. But you have no right to be a Chinaman; because you are only a Chinaman.' This is probably the highest point to which the German culture has risen. [10]

In his *Autobiography*, Chesterton gives a tempered example of his patriotic ideal as an antidote to imperialistic excess:

To us it seemed obvious that Patriotism and Imperialism were not only not the same thing, but very nearly opposite things. But it did not seem obvious, but very puzzling, to the great majority of healthy patriots and innocent Imperialists. . . . I have always felt it the first duty of a real English patriot to sympathize with the passionate patriotism of Ireland; that I expressed it through the worst times of her tragedy and have not lost it in her triumph. [11]

Chesterton saw patriotism as not only the love of one's own county, but also the respect for the love that other peoples have for their own countries. This rendered him at odds with his own countrymen over Ireland as well as with the position of England in the Boer War. He had the ability to see things not only through his own narrow, subjective interests, but also through the interests of other nations. For him, a world of patriotic nations did not have to imply a world of imperialistic, warring nations. You could love your own neighborhood without wanting to see the neighborhood across town destroyed.

One biographer, Michael Coren, speaks about Chesterton's identification of Germany with excessive nationalism:

His (Chesterton's) fear and hatred of Protestant Prussia and the larger Germany was intense; and had been long before the 1914 war. For Gilbert and Belloc the steady increase in German influence was an international evil, especially as it was to the direct detriment of Catholic France. There was no chance of the army ever accepting Gilbert for military service, and his endeavors to join up must be viewed in their true light; the quixotic romantic, not the unworldly fool. [12]

Nevertheless, solidarity as expressed through patriotism has less to do with identification with officialdom than with a commonality and regard for one's fellow people. Chesterton felt that to see how patriotism would be made manifest in a nation, one must look to the character of the people. The "people" in this instance refers to both the local and national levels, thus determining the mark of the nation as a whole. Coren describes Chesterton's particularly high regard for the character of the people of Poland:

> Gilbert had long been fascinated with Poland and its problems. Here was a large, vibrant Catholic country in between the giants of Germany and Russia; it was a victim state, a valiant state. He received the opportunity of visiting Warsaw in 1927, a guest of the P.E.N. Club. . . . If Gilbert was anxious to see Poland, Poland was even more anxious to see him. He was treated as if he were a royal visitor, a representative of the culture which Poland was determined to identify itself with . . . Gilbert's inscription in the Polish P.E.N. Club album was the ringing 'If Poland had not been born again, all the Christian nations would have died.' It was hyperbole, but also an honest indication of his love for the country. [13]

In Chesterton's historical philosophy, he was noteworthy in his observation that apparent contradiction, or paradox, usually contained larger truths that could enhance one's understanding of history. For example, in *The Ballad of the White Horse*, the apparent defeat of Alfred's forces at the hands of the Danes is in fact a victory because the willingness of the patriots to die cheerfully incites the continued resistance of others and the eventual conversion of the enemy. In his book, *Paradox in Chesterton*, Hugh Kenner focuses on Chesterton's belief that reality cannot be adequately summed up in logical terms alone and describes why Chesterton's use of paradox was successful:

> The truth is that there is good and bad paradox, just as there is good and bad art, just as there are shut and open eyes. Chesterton uses paradox safely because he was first a contemplative and second an artist; first he saw and then he made. . . . What good and bad paradoxes possess in common is the shock derived from contradiction: paradox is contradiction, explicit or implied. [14]

The emphasis Kenner places on contemplation and artistic expression highlights the importance of imagination in the expression of Chesterton's philosophy of history. Chesterton takes the imaginative leap that paradoxical expression requires, joining together apparent contradictions so that the unexpected elements of history are made more coherent. At the same time he does not ignore the discontinuities and mysteries in history that point beyond reason. Kenner goes on to indicate that paradox is something whose ultimate object is praise because the source of reality is wonderful.

In contrasting verbal and metaphysical paradox he touches on this theme of discontinuity that Chesterton tries to represent in his historical writing.

> The object of verbal paradox, then, is persuasion, and its principle is the inadequacy of words to thoughts, unless they be very carefully chosen words. But the principle of metaphysical paradox is something inherently intractable in being itself; in the Thing. Its immediate object is exegesis: its ultimate object is praise, awakened by wonder. Paradox springs in general from inadequacy, from the rents in linguistic and logical clothing; paradoxy might be called the science of gaps.[15]

Metaphysical paradox comes from the incommensurability of words and reality. This is significant for Chesterton's philosophy of history because the reality of history is so complex—as complex as the myriad actions of the countless men and women involved. As Aristotle observed, history deals with particulars and science deals with universals. Thus, a science of history is impossible and instruments such as imagination and paradox are more suited to the framing of historical coherence.

Kenner further postulates that those who, like Chesterton, wish to see into the reality of things must respect a certain degree of mystery:

> The beginning of the metaphysical vision, then, is to see things: to see, and to see things, and accept them with their inherent mystery: which process may roughly be called seeing them with surprise.... His (Chesterton's) real concern is with a metaphysical art of wonder which he calls "the life of men and the beginning of the praise of God" [The Colored Lands, p.108] That is the beginning, and the refusal of humankind to be surprised—that is, to be aware—is the primary problem for him who would communicate his vision.[16]

The refusal of humankind to be surprised makes it necessary for a writer to call attention to meaning in the striking way that paradox provides. The skillful writer will use paradox to get the attention of his reader and to illustrate his point.

In commenting on *The Man Who Was Thursday*, Kenner touches on the historical when he points out two ultimate patterns: the linear pattern of a man's life, which has the character of a story, and the cyclical pattern represented by the wheel and identified with Eastern philosophies. The cyclical pattern ignores the individual person and subsumes him or her into an impersonal non-teleological reality. This idea is what Chesterton perceptively noted to be the enemy of St. Thomas Aquinas in the person of Siger de Brabant and his championing of the agent intellect.[17]

Kenner goes on to point out Chesterton's realization that this emphasis on the personal in history is the natural result of a personal reality behind history:

> The reconciliation of that antagonism between him who scoffs and him who worships is accomplished in The Man Who Was Thursday; for the antagonist of them both turns out to be the leader of them both. He is like the cosmic man of so much quasi-mystical speculation: the stupendous figure through whose limbs circle the stars. In him is transcended the isolation of soul from soul, which begets both loneliness and its blood-brother courage. The cosmos has the pattern of a man which is one of its two traditional ultimate patterns: the other being the wheel, the unending cycle. The serpent with its tail in its mouth, which Chesterton also perceived and abominated, summing it up through countless scattered passages in the restless, formless patterns of Turkish carpets, the restless, pointless cycle of Nirvana, and the annihilistic self-contemplation of the East. The cosmos has become a man, a man of will and energy and fantastic beauty, a man and therefore a cross. And when, in the final sentences of The Man Who Was Thursday, the last mask is torn off the face of Nature, there is displayed the older face of God: "Can ye drink of the cup that I drink of? [18]

Like Kenner, Quentin Lauer observes Chesterton through a philosophical lens and concludes that Chesterton saw natural reason alone as inadequate for coming to terms with the totality of reality. Like Kenner, Lauer also emphasizes the truth of Chesterton's conclusions over the mechanics of his thinking. He shows that Chesterton's artistic intuitive powers enabled him to have a more truth-filled understanding of history.

> Chesterton's view of philosophy—even his use of the term—differs considerably from the more technical understanding of the term when it is employed by some professional philosophers, for whom the term "philosophy" is reserved for an inquiry that is restricted to the purely natural function of reason; for Chesterton the merely natural could never be adequately human. In Chesterton's view, because reason functioning purely naturally—assuming as its advocates presumably do that reasoning is a function of nature and not uniquely a function of spirit—cannot come to terms with the totality of reality. A philosophy grounded in purely natural reasoning, therefore, cannot but be inadequate, even as philosophy. None of which prevents him, incidentally, from putting enormous stress on reason and rationality. In so doing, however, he puts far less stress on the mechanics of narrowly logical thinking than he does on the truth of the conclusions arrived at by a thinking, which is adequately rational; we might call this the objective rationality of what is thought, as distinct from the subjective rationalization of the thinking process. Here it is that Chesterton's conviction that reasoning can never be simply "doing what comes naturally" is of such extraordinary importance. [19]

Lauer also points out Chesterton's emphasis on human conduct, noting that he was not only concerned with truth as it is known, but also truth as it shapes the lives of particular persons. Lauer finds this to be a characteristically Victorian aspect of Chesterton's writing.

It seems clear from this that Chesterton would naturally emphasize what is *done* in history as much as what is *thought*. For him, man is a spiritual unity who cannot be split into a Manichean duality of good spirit and bad body. This is one of Chesterton's cardinal insights into Thomism and its importance in establishing the Catholic intellectual framework that was open enough to take in all of reality and not just a partial view:

> Still there was one conviction characteristic of the Victorian age that stayed with Chesterton and did much to form his way of life. Like Mathew Arnold, the last and most skeptical of them, who expressed their basic idea in its most detached and philosophical form, they held that conduct was three-fourths of life. There was no question in Chesterton's mind that what we are is extremely important, but he was also quite well aware that it is in what we do that we become what we are—and this bespeaks ethics (or morality) as the cardinal concern of Chesterton that led him back to religion.
>
> It is important to emphasize this concern in Chesterton if we are not to be misled by Marshall McLuhan's characterization (or caricature) of Chesterton in the Introduction to Hugh Kenner's profoundly perceptive book, Paradox in Chesterton, as a "metaphysical moralist, who, because presumably he was concerned with contemplating a world he had not made, was not concerned with shaping the minds of human beings and thus, even if only indirectly, shaping a world in which human beings live. [20]

Lauer later speaks of Chesterton's inclusion of mind and will—or head and heart—in Christian art. This duality, like that of body and spirit, is another instance of Chesterton's ability to hold seemingly oppositional realities at the same time, and give each its respective value, instead of collapsing into a reductionist monism:

> It is not without significance . . . that Christian art is richly theological, thus speaking to both head and heart in telling its theological story. It was this story that he saw spelled out all over the face of Britain as its medieval heritage. [21]

Chesterton's artistic nature seems to compel him to always make his images more clear and more sharply outlined. When he saw two contrasting images, he preferred to reveal them both with all their respective vividness, instead of highlighting one and dispensing with the other. In *The Everlasting Man*, he talks about this need for clarity:

> I do not believe that the past is most truly pictured as a thing in which humanity merely fades away into nature, or civilisation merely fades away into barbarism, or religion fades away into mythology, or our own religion fades away into the religions of the world. In short, I do not believe that the best way to produce an outline of history is to rub out the lines. I believe that, of the two, it would be far nearer the truth to tell the tale very simply, like a primitive myth about a man who made the sun and stars or a god who entered the body of a sacred monkey. [22]

Chesterton's writings also provoked controversy during his own lifetime. One contemporary critic, William Scott, objected to the adversarial tone with which Chesterton wrote of his contemporaries:

> The one thing which stands out with the greatest prominence in the writings of Mr. Chesterton is that of his pugnacity. Mr. Chesterton is a born fighter. He is first and foremost a propagandist. Nothing seems to delight him more than to find an adversary who will face him toe to toe. . . . Mr. Chesterton likes Bernard Shaw. He considers him as a man with a system of thought and always consistent in his expression. . . . Mr. Chesterton has attacked Kipling for his lack of patriotism; Tolstoi for the meagerness of his simple life; Ibsen, for his strange inconsistencies in the portrayal of character; George Moore, for his perpetual posing. [23]

It is interesting to note that Scott mentions Chesterton's criticism of Kipling's lack of patriotism. At the time, Kipling was an icon of British imperialism. For Chesterton, it was not possible to be at the same time an imperialist and a true patriot because a genuine love of one's country would imply a respect for others' love for their own country, as he described in *The Everlasting Man*.

In another passage, Scott further attacks Chesterton as being a childish writer:

> Mr. Chesterton looks upon literature as a boy looks upon his toys—something to make noise with. He believes that the child life is the normal life and the child loves are the normal loves. [24]

However, Scott seems to contradict himself because he later complains that Chesterton is too old, in the sense of being conservative and out of step with many of his modern contemporaries:

> Another objection which may be made against Mr. Chesterton is that he is too young and too old. He is like a David going out against a Goliath, and the question is a debatable one whether he carries any pebble for his sling. He has boisterous confidence, but how about his muscle?

He seems too aged in his opinions to suit many of the moderns. He is extremely conservative. [25]

Unlike Kenner and Lauer who both understood Chesterton's appreciation for concrete realities, Scott fails to perceive that Chesterton was conservative precisely because he did not want to get rid of what was valuable, and because his philosophy was anchored in enduring truths. Chesterton seems to fall outside the political categories because he focuses on the nature of things, which remain true *regardless of local conditions.* In this sense, Chesterton is indeed child*like* in that he appreciates things for what they are without the distortions of seeing them through the colored lenses of political ideology.

Insofar as the label of conservative implies a desire to maintain the status quo, Chesterton does not fit into this rather narrow category. In important respects he was at odds with the established policies of his own time. Being a Distributist, Chesterton called for the redistribution of the means of production and land at a time when 75% of all land in the United Kingdom was owned by a tiny minority, mostly aristocratic. This is an example of one of the ways in which Chesterton was actually quite a progressive.

While Scott seems to have misread Chesterton on several key points, he did accurately understand that Chesterton did not state something without believing it to be true:

> Mr. Chesterton has persistently declared that his statements must be taken as expressing his complete convictions.... In his books we may trace various changes of thought, but they are changes which he has himself pointed out, and are chiefly upon minor matters. He does not say a thing because he believes it to be catchy and paradoxical, but because he believes it to be profoundly true. Perhaps one of the reasons why he likes Bernard Shaw is because Mr. Shaw has been strongly attacked for his use of the paradox. [26]

Another interesting contemporary account of Chesterton comes from W.R. Titterton, who was a deputy editor under him at the *New Witness*, the newspaper of Chesterton's late brother, Cecil Chesterton. In his biography, *G.K. Chesterton: A Portrait*, Titterton recalls the tremendous personal influence that Chesterton had on him. One significant lesson Titterton learned from him was the value of common things and ordinary people. We can roughly describe common things as local and accessible as opposed to foreign and exotic. This emphasis on the value of local and common things is tied to Chesterton's Distributism, a philosophy that Titterton also came to appreciate under Chesterton's influence. Distributism emphasizes that every person can best develop where there is local ownership of property, and that the ownership be as widely distributed as possible. In contrast to Distributism, Socialism tends to centralize ownership among a few, even if those few are hidden under the name of the State. Titterton sums up Chesterton's influence on him:

> Let me rather hint at the effect that G.K.C. had upon me. I mean apart from the tremendous fact that he, more than any other man, persuaded me to be a Catholic, and he more even than Belloc turned me from a Socialist into a Distributist. He taught me the value of common things and ordinary people; he taught me to understand for the first time the meaning of democracy. . . . He taught me to fight without rancour, and to love the enemy while I hated his creed. And, from first to last, he amazed me, overpowered me with his innocence and humility. [27]

Later in his biography, Titterton points out two of Chesterton's seminal thoughts about Jesus Christ. Christ died seemingly overwhelmed by unconquerable forces. In this sense, he is the same as the patriot who defends his local love in the face of a larger aggressor. Chesterton's God could sympathize with the Saxons fighting against the Danes in Chesterton's *Ballad*. Titterton also points out that Chesterton's God has a sense of humor:

> There were two things of which he (Chesterton) was really proud. One was that we have a God Who died with His back to the wall. The other was that we have a God with a sense of humour. Well, humour springs from a sense of proportion, and the Architect of the Universe must have that. But what makes it blossom into laughter is love.
> G.K.C. once pointed out that Our Lord founded His Church on a pun: 'Thou art Peter (rock) and upon this rock will I build my Church.' And he said elsewhere that there were times when Our Lord hid His face or went away from men. And he wonders if that which He hid, He Who never hid His tears, was His mirth.
> And I think that when Belloc wrote: 'There's nothing worth the wear of living save laughter and the love of friends,' he had much the same idea. For laughter and the love of friends shall flood the courts of Heaven. [28]

The notion that Christ hid his face from men to hide his mirth was from Chesterton's book, *Orthodoxy*. The idea that laughter and friends will fill the courts of Heaven was from *The Ballad of the White Horse*, in which Chesterton also talks about a God who sees humor in the world because he is the Creator and has the sense of proportion. In the *Ballad*, Chesterton speaks of the God "who loves, yet laughs among the swords . . ."[29] These different facets of Chesterton's understanding of God shed light on how he understood God's providence regarding the actions of mankind throughout history.

It is interesting to juxtapose Titterton's biographical memoirs with the later perspective of biographer, Michael Ffinch. Ffinch discusses the important reactions Chesterton had in relation to the historical events of his time. One significant example was the question of women's suffrage (and feminism in general). As with other special interest movements, Chesterton found within feminism a mixture of truth and falsehood. He maintained that in more radical feminism, there was a seeming exchange of women's virtues with men's vices. In fact, he pointed out that women already exercised an incalculable influence on history through their role in society:

> ... When he had been interviewed by Maude Cherton Braby for the Tribune, Chesterton had admitted that women's suffrage was the only topic in the universe on which he had not come to a decision. He thought that if the mass of women wanted it, then it should be given, but he feared that political rights might 'simply give to women the same snappy, scientific civilization of men, make them more pert, more sophisticated, more fond of pretending to knowledge', and this would be simply throwing away their virtues and giving them men's vices instead ... She (woman) was, of course, in every way equal to a man. The nonsense about woman being man's intellectual inferior, Chesterton would dismiss with his hand, or rather with his foot. The vast majority of men, he said, were guided by women all their lives. [30]

For Chesterton, something that remains true to its own nature will have the best chance for success and the greatest effect on its surroundings. It is interesting to note that in his book, *What's Wrong With The World*, Chesterton toiled with the question of women's suffrage because he found that, at his time, few women were interested in it.[31] He did not, however, disparage the importance or the influence of women throughout history. To the contrary, in the essays he wrote on women, particularly in *What's Wrong With The World*, Chesterton defends the nobility of womanhood, albeit with a tone more typical of his time.

Ffinch cites another causative agent in history that Chesterton discussed at length, namely the Catholic Church. He comments that the Catholic Church has managed to exercise its influence in history by remaining true to its nature and not changing with the times for its most pivotal points:

> By the middle of October (1921) the papers were, as Chesterton said, 'full of headlines about the Church Congress'. In his editorial on 21 October he commented on Lord Dawson's statement that 'Christian morality need no longer restrain us in the matter of "birth control", and as many newspapers had rallied behind it, saying that if the Church was to live, it must 'move with the times', or, as some put it, 'must move with the world'. Chesterton said he had much more time for men who recognized Christian morals as Christian, and denied them as such, than he had for those who called themselves Christians and then set

about 'brazenly betraying the Christian's vital point of honour'. It was one tiresome, tireless, all-destroying and indestructible piece of nonsense to say that all things should be judged by whether they are suited to our industrial cities. Nothing could be more false to history, he argued, than the statement that, if the Church is to live, it must move with the times.[32]

As Chesterton states in his book, *Alarms and Discursions* (1910), "No one worth calling a man allows his moods to change his convictions; but it is by moods that we understand other men's convictions." [33] Chesterton maintained throughout his career that one cannot base one's convictions on mere fancy. In fact, it was the consistency of Chesterton's ideas as well as his efforts to better understand the beliefs of others that were among the defining characteristics that led even his opponents to respect him.

In his study of Chesterton, Ian Boyd brings to light an interesting aspect of Chesterton's historical philosophy. He states that Chesterton somewhat naively championed situations when a king or authority figure in a nation could "represent an easy solution to the difficult problems of modern politics."[34] However, Boyd interprets the authority figure role foreseen by Chesterton in a rather exaggerated manner:

> The political role he (Chesterton) imagines for the king (monarchy) is perhaps harmless enough. And since he is supposed to represent genuine authority, it is probably unfair to call him a Fascist figure. But the way in which he combines contempt for the parliamentary government with a fondness for authoritarian action does suggest the kind of Fascist solution which some of Chesterton's followers were accused of advocating shortly after his death.[35]

While it is true that Chesterton was somewhat romantic about monarchy, his consistent defense of the common man and of democracy leaves little doubt that he would *not* be in favor of any excessively authoritarian solution to political problems. Poems such as *Lepanto* and *The Ballad of the White Horse* show Chesterton's understanding of a monarchy capable of bringing out the best in its subjects while refraining from any totalitarian tendencies. Chesterton saw that limited monarchy and democracy could coexist in a complementary fashion.

Like Lauer, Boyd highlights Chesterton's ability to see man and history in a multi-dimensional form. The talent is derived from Chesterton's artistic capabilities. In his essay "Philosophy in Fiction", Boyd speaks about Chesterton's view of life as a symbolic narrative:

> The implication of Chesterton's view is that the whole of human life is made up of an unending series of hieroglyphs which it is the business of the allegorist to select and interpret. There is no question of a thesis

which can be presented alternatively as a symbolic narrative or as a discursive argument. . . . This may be why Chesterton speaks of the artistic mind as one that 'sees things as they are in a picture'. And finally, this may be why in one of the later novels, the central character makes a claim for an entirely symbolic view of life: 'I doubt,' Gabriel Gale says, 'whether any of our actions is really anything but an allegory. I doubt whether any truth can be told except in parable' (The Poet and the Lunatics: Episodes in the Life of Gabriel Gale)[36]

Chesterton did not see life as a discursive argument because a discursive argument is a linear, logical movement from a premise to a conclusion. In contrast, a symbolic narrative is a story in which the events and the characters have meaning in both the figurative and literal senses. In this way, a person's life is richer and deeper than any discursive argument. The element of context is lost in discursive arguments because they are abstracted and focused on the syllogistic movement from premise to conclusion, whereas life is layered and densely arranged like a picture.

This notion has a direct correlation to the reason why locality is such a central theme in Chesterton's artistic and philosophical vision. This is because it is only in dealing with particular places, customs and habits of life that a story can emerge. By their very nature, stories are not abstract: No one writes a story about characters without any character.

Chesterton's vision and insight are determining factors in his place in literary history. Like all writers, however, he was not without his weak points. In his essay entitled "A Brief Survey of Chesterton's Works", Dudley Barker proffers his own view on Chesterton's historical role:

> He is accepted as the best English aphorist of our century. His little priest, Father Brown, ranks among the dozen best-known detectives of fiction. In addition to all that, of course, he wrote a huge amount of ephemeral, tired, worthless prose, and a very great deal of nonsense. . . . And the poetry. Nobody, I imagine, would call Chesterton a great poet.[37]

Barker acknowledges Chesterton's talent for aphorism—his ability to capture an element of truth in a brief statement. Barker also points out Chesterton's abilities to summarize many particulars in one general truth. He further acknowledges Chesterton's voluminous output, which stems from his journalistic vocation and his own appetite for expression. Yet, like other critics, he points out the weaker link of poetic talent.

With regard to Chesterton's historical philosophy, Barker writes about Chesterton's rejection of the Whig theory of history:

> Chesterton attacked Wells' theme of the steady betterment of mankind in The Everlasting Man, essentially a Christian view of history, centered around the brief life on earth of Jesus. In a sense it is the sequel to

his earlier Orthodoxy, the completion of his journey from non-belief to complete and immovable religious conviction.[38]

Chesterton saw H.G. Wells' outline of history as a poor match for the abundant evidence of the past as well as contemporary times. For Chesterton, history was not a linear movement of constant improvement but rather a story with setbacks, victories, and tragedies, all with a dramatic center in the Incarnation.

In his book, Barker also points out the parallels between Orwell and Chesterton:

> Chesterton saw (In The Napoleon of Notting Hill), as George Orwell later saw, the approaching danger of the authoritarian State. But Chesterton's vision of the future was the antithesis of Orwell's. . . . Chesterton, with his innate optimism, believed, as Orwell did not, that eventually human beings would throw off the chains of the authoritarian State—communism, as he saw it, for by the time fascism arose he was too old and too prejudiced to recognize it for what it was. In Chesterton's vision of the future, Big Brother does not exist.[39]

Barker's observation directly contrasts with Boyd's assertion that Chesterton's political and historical philosophy left the door open to authoritarian tendencies. Instead, Barker finds that Chesterton's optimism moved him to the belief that an authoritarian state could never completely subjugate human beings. But Barker fails to give Chesterton credit for his even wider historical vision. Chesterton understood that the authoritarian state of modern times was quite similar to the one that had flourished in England some four hundred years before. This is fully in evidence in his book, *The Napoleon of Notting Hill*.

Chesterton derived his broad understanding precisely because he did not subscribe to the Whig theory of history. In its place, he saw human nature involved in a great struggle that found its definitive expression in the life of Christ. This is why he believed that the Incarnation and Christianity were at the heart of history.

Later in his book, Barker reiterates Chesterton's notion of the struggle and eventual triumph of good over evil as evidenced in *The Man Who Was Thursday*, and also in the novel's treatment of the authoritarian state. He points out that it foreshadowed events that were to occur later in the twentieth century.

> This last section of the book (The Man Who Was Thursday) is simultaneously a representation of the struggle between good and evil in which evil is at last defeated, and a symbolic construction of the authoritarian State of the twentieth century which, already by 1905, Chesterton perceived in the future, and of which he uttered this terrifying warning.[40]

Chesterton emphasized the eminent role of the individual person throughout history, implying a spiritual force with vision and a capability of foregoing immediate satisfaction for the sake of some greater good. In this he resembled the philosophy of the Persian poet, Omar Khayyam, who wrote in *The Rubayatt* that the wise man is one who knows how to forego present pleasure for future gain. Chesterton persistently maintained that the dedication and sacrifice of individuals were paramount to historical progress.

In his book, *G.K. Chesterton & Hilaire Belloc: The Battle Against Modernity*, Jay P. Corrin cites the importance of the individual citizen for Chesterton:

> Chesterton believed that the individual citizen could do something to modify the tendency towards the servile state; once the plutocratic pressure was removed, or even eased, the appetite for private ownership would revive.[41]

Chesterton saw that the individual without overwhelming financial needs would be more disposed to working with others toward a common good since he would lack the burden of the impersonal force that money often presents. Extremely wealthy people are often capable of exerting their influence over great distances without the need for personal persuasion. Oftentimes their influence is commensurate with the impersonal means and ceases to be effective when their money is gone.

When Chesterton talks of plutocratic pressure being removed, i.e., when the rule of a small group of rich men is eliminated, then the desire for private ownership would naturally follow. This appetite implies a human nature that would seek to be creative and require material means to exercise this creativity. The stability of property provides the long-term security within which the person's creativity can be realized.

Corrin goes on to expound upon Chesterton's idea of the model community:

> Chesterton's reform called for the development of a model Distributionist community.... It was to be a family-oriented society of diffused property in which every man could direct the affairs of his own life, construct his own environment, eat what he liked, and wear what he pleased. The ownership of small-scale property would provide excitement to life, help inculcate responsibility through personal choice and introduce the challenge of being creative within limits. Chesterton proposed that the state initiate special differential taxation so as to discourage the sale of small property to big proprietors and facilitate the purchase of land by the propertyless, destroy primogeniture, protect and subsidize needed experiments in small property holdings by tariffs if necessary, and sponsor educational programs designed to encourage

handicrafts and farming. Lastly, workers were urged to organize special guild organizations which ultimately would buy out the capitalists and exercise cooperative control of all industry.[42]

The family orientation stresses the local decentralized element that is crucial to providing sustained movement toward common goods and goals. There is a natural, common orientation of people who live in the same home and neighborhood. The implication this kind of local focus has for Chesterton's historical vision is that his philosophy of history tends toward an emphasis on a particular place, since this is where man's creative and spiritual force is launched. For instance, Chesterton is well known to have pointed out that Rome was not loved because she was great, but rather that Rome was great because she was loved.

The Romans' emphasis on the goods of the hearth stands in contrast to the collective impersonalism of Carthage. Roman civilization in its prime spread order and humane growth while the Carthaginians were a short-term success but a long-term failure. Chesterton hoped to encourage through Distributism the deep local roots that would bear more enduring fruit, and saw that this kind of local fertilization was the difference between productive periods of history and those periods which may have appeared glamorous but which had no lasting consequence.

Like Barker, Christopher Hollis points to Chesterton's rejection of the Whig theory of history. However, in his book, *The Mind of Chesterton*, Hollis posits that Chesterton not only rejected but also provided a correction to the Whig theory:

> That is to say, it (Short History of England) justly corrects the Whig and Victorian history in whose eyes nineteenth-century stability was the solid, final achievement of man and all that leads up to it automatically to be praised. He justly insists ... on the price that was paid for the industrial revolution in the uprooting and degradation of the poor, and condemns the Victorians for the blind eye which they turned on this great evil.[43]

Hollis understands that Chesterton did not agree with the false optimism of the Victorians that was inaccurate precisely because it failed to see the evils of its own time. Hollis also pointed out that the Whig historical philosophy did not imply a human nature in need of continual reform but one that could be perfected in the present time.

Unlike the Whig view of history, Chesterton believed that human nature was indeed continually in need of returning to its true self. This reforming would take place with each new generation: The older one civilizing and humanizing the younger one, which would imply a history with a character not linear and upward moving, but reflective of each generation's particular successes and failures. Chesterton's view of history sees each historical period as a story with the character of an adventure and the unexpected. As he famously said' "your mother and father lie in wait to ambush you when you are born and you have no choice of who they will be." As it is for the individual, history will always have the character of the particular and the unrepeatable.

Like a story, history is the unfolding of the adventures of many unique persons with freedom. Each person's adventure story will unfold in a specific place and time. Chesterton saw that the story would be a poor one to the degree that its unfolding is subject to the attempted control of a few other persons. His dislike of the plutocrats was intense because he saw them as attempting to rewrite the many adventure stories into one controlled and boring tale.

Author Maisie Ward highlights Chesterton's development of the idea that history is a good story when it is composed of many small, good adventure stories:

> The attitude on the war, the personal love of his sovereign, both belonged to a social and political philosophy that Gilbert was slowly working out. One side of it found expression in The Napoleon of Notting Hill: the poetry of limitations, the belief in small nations and strict boundaries. Patriotism appeared to him not akin to Imperialism but its very opposite. The patriot loves his own country, the imperialist wants to swallow other countries. He opposed in the Boer War the imperialism of England and was entirely logical in opposing in the first world war the imperialism of Germany. He was never a pacifist but always an anti-imperialist patriot.[44]

For Chesterton, the imperialist was the plutocrat gone international. After rewriting all the local adventure stories, the imperialist's next task would be to rewrite the stories of the more distant neighbors.

Ward notes, as do other critics, Chesterton's opposition to his country's policy in South Africa and his agreement with his country's policy on the first World War. She sees the two views as consistent with his patriotism because Chesterton's love of his own locality did not make him hate other peoples' love of their own locality.

This paradoxical element in Chesterton's patriotism is noted in Joseph Pearce's monograph on Chesterton. In describing Chesterton's visit to Rome and his audience with the Pope in 1929, Pearce writes:

> He believed passionately that the central reality of Rome did not reside with Il Duce but with Il Papa. Fascism would fade away but the Pope would remain. Hence thousands of goose-stepping Blackshirts on the secular streets of Rome were not so powerful as a handful of Swiss Guards on the steps of St Peter's. The paradox pleased Chesterton immensely . . ."

Pearce goes on to quote a passage of Chesterton from The Resurrection of Rome:

> "And then I suddenly remembered that long ago, in my older days of scribbling, I had written a ridiculous story about Notting Hill; of which the joke was that a man might die for a little suburb as if for a holy city; and that I had equipped the men fighting for it with the same sort of halberds and heraldic colours. The man standing on the great stairway was, among a myriad other more important things, one of my own little dreams come true. And I realized with something rather like alarm at the coincidence, that the comparison might really have been pressed further. For the Guard of the Vatican City really was defending a place almost parochial in size though the reverse of parochial in importance. That here in the heart of Christendom, on the high place of the whole world, on a plane above all earthly empires and under the white and awful light that strikes on an eternal town, was really a model state no larger than Notting Hill." [45]

This episode shows the development of the idea that defending one's own small home has an importance that is anything but small. This is because only those who defend a place because they love it can fight with the tenacity that results in an enduring effect. Examples of this type of loyal defense would be the American Revolution, the Scots at Bannockburn and the Spanish during Napoleon's Iberian Campaign.

Naturally, Chesterton's observation pertains to a transcendental institution with a divine founder, but his insight is nevertheless analogously true for all the local loves that provide the impetus for enduring structures. Nations born on a huge scale fade quickly, whereas nations that grow from a smaller origin tend to last. The empire founded on the seven hills endures for a thousand years, with its effect lasting even longer. On the other hand, the empire founded on the grand designs of the Bolsheviks lasts for seventy years. Both Napoleon's grand designs and the Third Reich followed a similar pattern.

Chesterton saw the deeper historical importance and lasting effect of the local patriot despite the immediate outcome of the battle. The local patriot's willingness to deny personal gain for the greater good of the mission plays a crucial role in history. Like Corrin, author Alzina Stone Dale points to this notion as pivotal in Chesterton's historical philosophy. This is evidenced in the following passage from her biography:

> The poem (The Ballad of the White Horse) is an expression of Chesterton's lifelong romantic conviction that it did not matter if an individual won so long as he fought as hard as he could and never gave up. As Chesterton saw it, victory had come again and again to the Christian side because, as it says in The Song of Roland, "Christians are right

and pagans are wrong," and because Christians keep struggling even when they are defeated. The whole point of using Alfred as an English Christian hero was that he "would dare anything for the faith, he would bargain in anything except the faith," by which Chesterton meant that Alfred took his mission—not himself—seriously. Therefore, the vital historical event, as Chesterton saw it, was not the great victory at Ethandune, but the baptism of Danish Guthrum. His baptism, along with his chiefs, ensured that although a century later there was a Danish king ruling in England, "he got the crown, but he did not get rid of the cross," and England remained a Christian realm.[46]

Chesterton believed that because the patriot fights out of a love, he has an effect that is as much personal as it is historical. He may die, but his witness has consequences of which even he is not fully aware. This unintended element in historical events points to a transcendent author of the adventure stories that make up history.

Dale also points out that Chesterton was not using historical facts in the *Ballad*:

> Although Chesterton used stories not considered historical, Alfred was a historical king, so this poem gave him a chance to combine his pictorial and historical imaginings into a unified whole . . .[47]

However, I would argue along similar lines that I have put forth already, namely that Chesterton told the history of the Saxon resistance to the Danes in the only really effective historical way. Since the particular details are not the most important statements to be made about history, the best way to convey the truth of that particular historical episode is to tell it in the form of a story. It is not necessarily the arbitrary facts about Alfred and his contemporaries that comprise the essential lessons of the tale, but rather the use made of their personal freedom and its consequences.

Regarding history, another great strength of Chesterton was his clear-sighted, direct, and uncynical view of the world. This gave him an insight similar to the child in the tale of *The Emperor's New Clothes*. In his chapter entitled "The Defence of Notting Hill", writer Garry Wills notes the influence of Chesterton's perspective on his historical ideas:

> It is difficult to overestimate the naïveté and purity of Chesterton's first Liberalism. He approached the assumptions of his youth with that demand for theoretical consistency which we find at every stage of his development. There was a strange glamour about the ideas which hovered beneficently over the world into which he was born—progress, enlightenment, expansion and freedom. Chesterton took what was vaguely assumed and sharply asserted it—that Rousseau had revealed men's equality to a world which had never heard the

news, that Napoleon shattered a universal tyranny and freed the nations. Liberalism was to him both a creed and a party; he made no distinction between them. [48]

Wills points out that Chesterton saw things in clear outlines. He viewed Rousseau and Napoleon as almost symbolic figures, and grasped their message while separating it from the character of the men. Like Boyd, Wills understands the congruence between Chesterton's clear-sighted observation and his tendency to think symbolically and allegorically.

In the *Ballad*, Chesterton states that the use of legend is to telescope history. In writing that poem, he had his three protagonists, Colin, Mark, and Alfred, symbolize in their persons the three defining influences of Celtic, Roman, and Saxon culture on the formation of England. It is therefore not surprising that in his early days he would see the forest but not pay attention to individual trees.

Wills also points out that Chesterton sometimes lacked clarity on the concrete details of how his ideal liberalism would be put into practice:

> As Chesterton learned a little of real politics, and felt the foundations of his Liberalism crumbling, his reaction was like that of the new theologians who thought Christianity would be washed away unless they rescued it: he invented a series of "higher Liberalisms.". . . . Chesterton continued to support the "higher Liberalism" of The Wild Knight and Thursday—the belief that God gives each man a secret dispatch for battle and rebellion in the world. From the time when aesthetes and nihilists seemed, in his youth, to control the stars, Chesterton considered human virtue a rebellion against the Prince of this World. Man is in exile and under tyranny—but the tyranny is not from outside him. Man's real fight is against original sin; and this revolution is a restoration.[49]

But it seems to me that Chesterton was more interested in the truth of the ideal, and did not worry too much about its practical implementation, because he had a belief that all causes are essentially spiritual. This means that ideas are the most practical things of all in the long term because only they serve to motivate people.

Chesterton maintains that if one gets the principles right and they are then taken to heart, there will be myriad ways in which to implement them. The ideals will reflect the qualities of the people of the localities that implement them. I think that is why, if the goods being pursued are true goods, then they may be given different embodiments in different parts of the world. For instance, Spanish and Irish people can affirm the same goods, but will do so in different ways.

In writing about Chesterton's view of historical and political theories, Wills observes the following:

As always, his ideas first shaped themselves into colors and narrative, and in 1904 he wrote the book which he always considered his basic statement of political belief—The Napoleon of Notting Hill.

> Here, at the springs of his thought, we see clearly that Chesterton's democracy transcended particular political forms. Adam Wayne, the suburban Napoleon, has a thirst for diversification, for hierarchies and liveries and separate societies. But these are not advanced as parts of a system, of a neo-feudalism. Rather they indicate a revolt against the voracious appetite for Systems. He realized that the mechanical, utilitarian, quantitative schemes were even more the danger of twentieth-century politics than they had been in the Victorian era. Fascism, Communism, and Socialism have borne out that judgment.[50]

Chesterton disliked systems for their own sake because they are by definition restrictive of the reality that confronts any specific group of people. For example, the English experience in the Northern counties differs from the English experience in the Southern counties. As such, Londoners are different than Yorkshire men, and an attempt to control them all under the same scheme is not productive.

Chesterton wanted to have maximum diversification and to let the order in the diversity come from spiritual principles that are internal as opposed to systematic principles applied from without. It seems clear that Chesterton's understanding of how groups of men should organize comes from his beliefs about human nature. With regard to the manner in which this diversification could be unified within patriotic and nationalistic boundaries, Wills notes the following:

> All of Chesterton's writings during and after the war were impelled by patriotism and based upon his own belief in nationalism. The Napoleon of Notting Hill contained Chesterton's basic argument for the nation: the fact that the works of man should be expressions of his character. Chesterton no longer believed that the vote, or any other piece of republican machinery, could guarantee this expression; he would contend, before long, that without personal ownership men cannot stamp matter with their spirit. But the war made him realize that unless the nation is sealed with a separate character it is not worth defending. That is the reason he insisted on a moral judgment in the war.[51]

Chesterton also made an interesting comparison between the influence of voting and property ownership. According to him, the vote is too easily manipulated by wealthy people and by plutocrats. Thus, private property stands in contrast as an unmediated from of expression. Unlike the vote, property is subject to the constructive impulses of individual persons. A man can cast his vote and feel he has had some little influence, but when he decorates his house and plants his garden, he has a decidedly more immediate and pervasive influence on his life.

Chesterton also liked to talk about the homely details of personal life. It is not insignificant that garden plots and other such private expressions figure prominently in many of his stories. It is the defense of these closely-held gardens that inspire people to fight for their community and ultimately their nation. Wills is correct in seeing a connection between Chesterton's nationalism and the character of the people, as well as with the expressions of personal property.

This evolution from a naive understanding of classical liberalism to a more comprehensive view of reality demonstrates how Chesterton was guided above all by his understanding of how men really behave. He thinks in specific colors and shapes as is appropriate to his artistic nature. As a result, he consistently gives embodiment to his ideas through his literary creations.

As he grew in experience, Chesterton kept the ideals that he had attached to liberalism, but saw that neither liberal nor socialist, nor even conservative approaches were wholly adequate because the one element they all had in common was a very human tendency to misuse authority.

In developing the idea of subsidiarity, the French writer, Chantal Millon-Delsol, gives a detailed analysis of how the anti-authoritarian principle would have to be built into the political order so that this common human tendency could be kept from destroying any society. In her ground-breaking book on the principle of subsidiarity in European history, Millon-Delsol notes the following:

> L'idée de subsidiarité . . . vise à dépasser l'alternative entre le libéralisme classique et le socialisme centralisateur, en posant différemment la question politico-sociale. Elle légitime philosophiquement les droits-libertés, et revient aux sources des droits-créances supposés avoir été détournés de leur justification première. Elle parvient a l'accord viable d'une politique sociale et d'un Etat decentralisé, en payant cet assemblage paradoxal de deux renoncements: elle abandonne l'égalitarisme socialiste au profit de la valeur de dignité; elle abandonne l'individualisme philosophique au profit d'une societé structurée et fédérée.[52]

Millon-Delsol develops the notion of subsidiarity in situating its most current form in the 19th century. This is interesting because it coincides to some extent with Chesterton's own period of political thought. She lays out the framework for an appropriate use of authority that coincides very much with the sort of ideals that Chesterton fleshed out in his literary works. Authority is only a tool to further the common good and has the character of service rather than control. Also, Millon-Delsol calls for the abandonment of socialist egalitarianism, rooted in the very liberalism Chesterton grew out of, and a valuing, or revaluing, of the individual whose dignity would be derived from a positive contribution to a well-structured, diverse society (the "common good") rather than from the pursuit of self-serving, individualistic goals.

Like Chesterton, Millon-Delsol admits that this paradoxical renunciation crucial to a decentralized state in which authoritarian power is limited, poses little appeal to the modern mind:

> L'idée de subsidiarité ne recueille guère d'écho chez les modernes. Elle rappelle un principe de droit administratif, donc relégué dans les manuels techniques. Plus généralement, elle est connue par les spécialistes et les amateurs de la doctrine sociale de l'Eglise: elle a revêtu sa forme actuelle au XIXe siècle, dans un contexte sociologique et polique que n'est plus. [53]

Chesterton foresaw the possibilities of service-oriented government. For instance, when King Alfred is in the old woman's hut asking for cakes, we see a supreme authority not arrogating to itself the privileges of its position, but rather taking on a role of service to the society that it is charged with protecting and developing. Although adamant that governing authority could not be an end unto itself, Chesterton, like Millon-Delsol, did not relegate it to an arbitrary secondary rank but rather to a well-studied, palliative role in amending that which is lacking in society. Millon-Delsol further points out that the justification for the existence of state authority is precisely derived from these societal needs:

> Faces aux diverses conceptions de l'authorité, celle-ci suppose la relégation de l'authorité au second rang, mais qu'il ne faudrait pas traduire par n'importe quelle secondarité.... Trois idées complémentaires se conjuguent pour exprimer l'idée de subsidiarité:
> L'authorité est seconde en ce qu'elle ne tire sa nécessité que du besoin d'une autre instance. Elle n'a pas de finalité propre ...
> L'authorité est supplétive parce qu'elle a pour premier rôle de pallier les insuffisances de la société, mais sans oeuvrer à sa place dans les domaines où elle se suffit. Elle justifie d'abord son existence par l'existence du besoin de l'instance sociale.
> Enfin, l'authorité joue un rôle subsidiare au sens de secours positif, qui peut aller au-delà des strictes insuffisances: cette fonction demeure la plus difficile à justifier et fut, depuis le XIXe siècle, largement controversée. En effet, l'authorité ne se contente pas de 'boucher les trous'.[54]

Like Wills, Millon-Delsol finds merit in the subjugation of the power of the state to that of the essential needs of the people. However, as she points out, this limitation does not merely imply a reactive bandaging of problems, but may instead roam into the rather nebulous zone of preventative care. As she says, the state cannot content itself with simply plugging up the holes as they appear on the scene.

Millon-Delsol further points out that the only legitimate universal task of the state is a diachronic one, namely to contribute to increasingly responsible personal action and to lessen its own coercive influence. Chesterton's stress of individual responsible action fits in very well with Millon-Delsol's vision of the state. The only time that Adam Wayne is ready to sacrifice his life is in defense of his local community of Notting Hill. This fits in with Millon-Delsol's understanding that an individual may sacrifice part of his or her autonomy for the common good, but only on his or her own initiative. The only way that the common good could be considered worthy of the sacrifice and efforts of many of the citizens would be if the state sought to diminish its own intervention and promote the personal initiative of an ever-greater number of its people. Millon-Delsol describes this notion in the following passage:

> Il (l'Etat) n'est pas dépositaire d'une oeuvre concernant le tout, parce que ce tout n'a qu'une existence abstraite, et ne peut rien vouloir pour lui-même comme tout, il n'est qu'un résultat et non une aspiration, La seule tâche universelle dont l'Etat peut à la limite se charger est une tâche historique: celle de contribuer à supprimer dans l'avenir sa propre intervention, et cette tâche coïncide avec le déploiement de plus en plus autonome des individualités. L'idée de bien commun représente ici une sort de chimère, ce qui serait une essence platonienne vue par le nominalisme. Le bien commun considéré comme un dessein rationnel, et justifié, suppose une société valant pour personne morale, laquelle par conséquent les individus pourraient à bon escient sacrifier une partie de leur autonomie. Le refus de l'individualisme fondateur légitimera l'idée de justice sociale dans la philosophie sociale néo-thomiste.[55]

Chesterton's writings rehearse in concrete form the results of a coercive state, and celebrate the flourishing that comes from the widest possible distribution of personal responsibility. Colin, Mark, and Alfred all contribute to the repulsion of the Danes, as do all the many individuals fighting for little Wessex. They do not fight under coercion, and their motivation springs from a realization that the Danes represent a monolithic destructive power unwilling to make personal distinctions.

Millon-Delsol also touches upon the paradoxical outcomes that proceed from a state which does not begin with true principles. A small group is incapable of promoting the common good of a large group because of the limitations of the human person. A person is limited in time and space and can only fruitfully exert control over himself. His influence on his surroundings is most productively exerted through constructive work and persuasion. This seems to be the philosophical support for local autonomy.

In her chapter: "Corporatisme ou déviance du principe de subsidiarité", ("Corporatism or the deviance from the principle of subsidiarity"), the author speaks of a "dérive fatale" or "fatal drift" from the notion of subsidiarity into the ideological systemization of the corporative ideal, as was the case with Mussolini and in Nazi Germany, and which the Catholic Church is trying to amend.[56] She states that:

> La nécéssité de l'intervention étatique provient de la prise en main par des organismes sociaux d'une authorité de coercition traditionellement dévolue à l'instance publique. Les organismes sociaux utiliseront cette authorité pour défendre leur intérêts catégoriels appelant ainsi un contrôle supérieur. Si le corporatisme prône au départ la non-ingérence de droit très vite, l'abandonner, c'est qu'il part de la certitude erronée qu'un groupe privé garantira à lui seule le bien commun, valeur publique et s'aperçoit très vite que, même si les privés peuvent participer à la réalisation du bien commun, seule l'instance suprême peut la garantir en dernier recours. Pour avoir conféré au départ un pouvoir trop grand aux corps, il doit plus tard développer d'une manière exponentielle le pouvoir de l'Etat, qu'il s'agissait de réduire. Il est victime, comme tant d'autres théories, du paradoxe des conséquences. [57]

Millon-Delsol maintains that when the state's influence over its citizens is not oppressive, individuals are more inclined to work toward the common good. This is similar to Corrin's emphasis on Chesterton's elaboration that the common good is best served when the state encourages private ownership and provides a fertile infrastructure and freedom-enhancing environment that fosters the productivity and contribution of its individual citizens.

Chesterton's defense of locality as pivotal in the historical development of nations, be it in its most elemental form of the family and neighborhood, or on the larger regional scale, has its source in his understanding that it was from these particular spheres that man's creative, spiritual and material forces are unleashed. Furthermore, it is within the particular localities of a people that commonly-held values are fostered. These values in turn determine the national character and its respective manifestations of patriotism and nationalism, the latter being in varying degrees a force for good or evil depending on the ideals of a people. As biographers and critics alike have elucidated, the emphasis on the individual and the locality, together with the determining influence of ideals, formed the foundations of Chesterton's philosophy of history.

2 Influences and Contemporaries

In order to understand fully Chesterton's own philosophy of history, it would be useful to place it in context with the historical philosophies of some of Chesterton's contemporaries. Chesterton's search for truth in the manifold accounts of history was both original and persistent. He did, however, react to and comment upon the written accounts of history by his predecessors.

In literary critic Harold Bloom's essay, "Poetry, Revisionism, Repression" he argues that every writer is reacting to the writers who came before him or her:

> A poem is not writing, but rewriting, and though a strong poem is a fresh start, such a start is a starting-again. In some sense, literary criticism has known always this reliance of texts upon texts . . . [1]

Bloom believes that each writer is filled with anxiety as a result of this reaction to his literary predecessors because he is afraid that he will not have anything original to say, and that whatever he does say will be unduly influenced by those who came before him. The strong poet in Bloom's understanding is someone who has a desire to assert himself:

> Strong poets present themselves as looking for truth in the world, searching in reality and in tradition, but such a stance, as Nietzsche said, remains under the mastery of desire, of instinctual drives. So, in effect, the strong poet wants pleasure and not truth; he wants what Nietzsche named as "the belief in truth and the pleasurable effects of this belief." No strong poet can admit that Nietzsche was accurate in this insight, and no critic need fear that any strong poet will accept and so be hurt by demystification.[2]

Chesterton is one such strong poet in that he searches for truth and takes pleasure in the world. However, for Chesterton truth and pleasure were compatible, since truth is the proper object of the intellect—it is pleasing to find the truth. Bloom's analysis tends to rely heavily on Freudian concepts, so he opposes pleasure and truth. But Chesterton's work shows that this is not necessarily the case. Just as Scott took pleasure in all the material trappings of history, so too did Chesterton take pleasure in wearing a cloak and carrying a sword cane, and dressing up as a cowboy with his friends.

The romanticism that preoccupies Bloom's literary criticism is something that Chesterton understood to be taking pleasure in the reality of things. Chesterton was also constantly being surprised by the realness of things. So, while Chesterton took pleasure in the real, he did not suffer from the disjunction that Bloom speaks of when he says that the strong poet wants pleasure and not truth.

Chesterton's view of tradition and individual freedom is a richer understanding of the interplay between old and new writers. This is because Chesterton did not have the insecurity that comes from being purely a critic, since his was a creative talent as well as an evaluative one. He was influenced by Sir Walter Scott and Hilaire Belloc in coming to an understanding of history, but he was also able to make his own contribution to historical understanding. This fact was exemplified in *The Everlasting Man* and in his historical poems.

Chesterton uses his imagination to give flesh to the historical truths that he acquired through his conversation with the past as well as the present. He conversed with the past when he read the writers who came before him, and he conversed with the present when he met with his contemporaries. Chesterton also displayed an artistic ability to bring these historical realities before the eyes of his readers with colorful images and a rhythmic language. He gave the story a beginning, a middle and an end. In this way, he showed himself to be in the tradition of Aristotle who stressed metaphor in his rhetorical works as a way of bringing reality before the eyes of others. This same philosopher understood the importance of a plot structure that limited the stream of history with a beginning, middle and end.

These considerations of metaphor and plot are aesthetic considerations because they deal with giving an appealing form to historical events. Chesterton the artist understood better than Belloc the historical polemicist or even Bloom the critical theorist that for most people, historical realities live most vibrantly in the imagination. Chesterton has a more complete view of writing and its possibilities since he is not only an analyzer but also a creator of new works that have an aesthetic character rather than an analytical one. In this sense, he is not only a strong poet in Bloom's sense, but he is also a rare combination of critical insight and artistic capability.

Like Belloc, Chesterton was also an essentialist. Both men adhered to the central point of essentialism that emphasizes essence over existence. Chesterton also saw that man's essence is incomplete and has a *status viatoris*. Being oriented toward fulfillment, man's nature requires justice and simplicity. In speaking about his friend Chesterton's character four years after his death, Belloc summed up his views in the following excerpt from his essay entitled "On the Place of Gilbert Chesterton in English Letters":

> The leading characteristic of Chesterton as a writer and as a man (the two were much more closely identified in him than in most writers) was that he was national. . . . The next characteristic was an extreme precision of thought . . . the third characteristic . . . is a unique capacity for parallelism. He continually illuminated and explained realities by comparisons. . . . (Fourth:) The structure upon which his work . . . had been founded was historical: but it was only in general historical; it was far more deeply and widely literary. . . . Fifth: Charity. He approached controversy, his delight, hardly ever as a conflict, nearly always as an appreciation, including that of his opponent. Lastly, there is that chief matter of his life and therefore of his literary activity, his acceptance of the Faith.[3]

Belloc points out that Chesterton's work has primarily a literary rather that historical structure. By contrast, Belloc was much more deeply immersed in the facts of history and less so in the structures of literature, which is to say that he understood that Chesterton was an artist, while he was not.

Belloc's friendship with Chesterton provided the latter with a great deal of historical background to which he could in turn give literary expression. One aspect of this literary expression was the ability to make appropriate comparisons. Chesterton shows this ability even in his understanding of Belloc's historical development:

> . . . Belloc's career began with the ideals of the Republican Club. To those who talk about ideals, but do not think about ideas, it may seem odd that both he and Eccles have ended as strong Monarchists. But there is a thin difference between good despotism and good democracy; both imply equality, with authority; whether the authority be impersonal or personal. What both detest is oligarchy; even in its more human form of aristocracy, let alone its present repulsive form of plutocracy. Belloc's first faith was in the impersonal authority of the Republic, and he concentrated on its return in the eighteenth century, but rather specially touching its military aspect.[4]

Chesterton sees the consistency in Belloc as he moved from republicanism to favoring a monarchy. Belloc understood the human need for authority as springing from man's nature, thereby showing again how much his thought depended on a prior philosophical understanding of man.

Chesterton's understanding of man influenced his distrust of plutocracy. He was wary of plutocracy because he understood it to be not anchored in man's nature but rather in a perversion of his nature: the desire to have a means as an end. For example, Chesterton saw money as a means to certain goods: food, clothing, shelter and the like. However, he also saw needs beyond those that are shared in common with animals, namely, the fulfillment of mind and heart, which are left empty by money.

But among the Very Rich you will never find a really generous man, even by accident. They may give their money away, but they will never give themselves away; they are egoistic, secretive, dry as old bones. To be smart enough to get all that money you must be dull enough to want it.[5]

Another trait Chesterton shared in common with Belloc was an appreciation for what the Greeks called "magnificence". It is a public virtue whereby the wealthy use their riches to give fitting public expression to the ideals held in common by all the people. Both men clearly saw that this virtue would take different forms depending on the locality in which it was manifest. For example, the gothic cathedrals of northern Europe would not be mirrors of the Romanesque ideals of the Mediterranean. Yet in both instances, there would be a fitting usage of money.

Their mutual appreciation for Greek "magnificence" lead to another common antipathy held by both men, namely a dislike of the "Teutonic" mentality. Biographer Raymond Las Vergnas noted that, ""Like Chesterton, the author of *Robespierre* (Belloc) has nothing but distrust for the German spirit."[6] Both men saw the "German spirit" as a complex problem because they considered it to be against the fulfillment of human nature. In the first place, it was coercive rather than freedom-enhancing. Secondly, it was destructive rather than constructive. And finally, they found it to be intent on control rather than promoting personal initiative.

Chesterton was not parochial enough to think that this German spirit did not infect the English as well. It was precisely this awareness that led him to oppose the Boer War.

Overall, both Belloc and Chesterton worked on similar historical problems, but approached them differently according to their respective temperaments. As Las Vergnas states:

> In Chesterton, exuberance predominates: lucidity in Belloc. . . . A taste for paradox seems, at first sight, to be common . . . yet paradox itself is found to be, in them, susceptible of very varied hues. Chesterton's shouts of laughter hardly suggest the guarded irony of Belloc. . . . The same problems fascinated them: the same ideal directed them: they met in the Communion of a self-same Faith. The Catholic Faith did indeed provide one and the self-same inspiration not only to their work, but to their very being.[7]

Chesterton always based his understanding of history on an understanding of man and man's nature. In this way, he is the opposite of an ideologue because he did not form theories or expectations and then force reality to coincide with them. Instead, he looked at what could be learned about human nature from observing particular men and women and allowed this to form his understanding. This is why he could say that even before recorded history, men behaved in generally the same way that they behaved during recorded history:

> In one sense it is a true paradox that there was history before history. But it is not the irrational paradox implied in prehistoric history; for it is a history we do not know. Very probably it was exceedingly like the history we do know, except in the one detail that we do not know it.[8]

Those who hold the Whig view of history suppose that man progressed from a rude and undeveloped state to a nearly perfect one. This approach fails to take into account the truth that human generations begin again and again, like plants, but do not progress linearly, as a train going up a hill.

H.G. Wells was a contemporary of Chesterton who held the view that history was a progression toward perfection. He did not take into account the objections that could be raised against a strictly evolutionary view of history. Even proponents of evolution as a biological theory have failed to account for the tendency of organisms to revert to the average rather than to pass on extraordinary traits in an infinite progression.

Chesterton formed his view of what men did before recorded history based on a pattern that refuses to systematize the world. For him, the world is more like an enormous garden in which there are many kinds of flowers and trees, all having their own particular characteristics. They are alike in that they all grow and attain their stature, and then decline. Each separate part of the garden can be likened to a locality, with its own terrain and climate. The way to make the garden succeed would be to keep each plant from interfering too much with its neighbors and make sure that all the plants are provided with what they need to flourish.

Wells's failure to recognize a human nature has implications for his understanding of history. Chesterton notes these implications in his chapter on Wells in *Heretics*:

> And an even stronger example of Mr. Wells's indifference to the human psychology can be found in his cosmopolitanism, the abolition in his Utopia of all patriotic boundaries.[9]

Because he doesn't recognize a human nature, Wells's philosophy tends toward a collapsing of differences. He envisions a world-state in which there are no wars. But Chesterton points out that a world state would result in many human beings making war on the world-state itself. Chesterton knows that human nature contains a paradox in the sense that it moves toward union as well as differentiation. He traces this ultimately to man's being made in the image of God:

> You can often get men to fight for the union; but you can never prevent them from fighting also for the differentiation. This variety in

the highest thing is the meaning of the fierce patriotism, the fierce nationalism of the great European civilization. It is also, incidentally, the meaning of the doctrine of the Trinity.[10]

In being patriotic, men are protecting their own individuality. Not wanting to be merged into a faceless, impersonal state, they nonetheless have desires for real union with their fellow men. The desire for local autonomy comes from this paradoxical structure that forms man's nature. This is why philosophically at least, Chesterton is in the tradition of St. Thomas, and Wells is in the tradition of William of Ockham. The nominalism that denies any enduring substance in the world would lead to a collapsing of distinctions that marks Wells's historical philosophy.

This collapsing of distinctions makes Wells an easy target for Chesterton's criticism, since his anti-essentialist philosophy renders all of his statements suspect. Nothing can be truly stated if there is nothing abiding in what we know. The historical realities of nationalism and patriotism find their origin in the human nature that Wells's philosophy does not recognize. On a deeper level, his philosophy negates his own knowledge. But on a more superficial level, it also negates his historical understanding.

In Chesterton's understanding, nations are the paradoxical expressions of human nature. They combine unity and differentiation in the same way that human nature does. They resist the collapsing of distinctions in the way that individual persons resist the leveling of their own personality. Wells acts as a kind of foil to Chesterton: In working out the flaws in Wells' philosophy, he was helped to clarify his own historical philosophy. In this sense, Wells had a good influence on Chesterton, which he most likely appreciated. The development of Chesterton's philosophy can be seen in the following excerpt from *The Everlasting Man*:

> People cannot easily get rid of the mental confusion of feeling that the foundations of history must surely be secure; that the first steps must be safe; that the biggest generalization must be obvious. But though the contradiction may seem to them a paradox, this is the very contrary of the truth. It is the large thing that is secret and invisible; it is the small thing that is evident and enormous.[11]

In contrast, Wells wanted to hold all of history in his mind through his use of an all-encompassing theoretical framework. Even the title of his book, *The Outline of History*, suggests an attempt to have a God-like grasp of a subject that is as densely-woven as human freedom. Chesterton doesn't see the need for such a vast, systematic framework because it would seem a waste of time to try to make human history take on the character of a mathematical proof. His famous remark in *Orthodoxy* about the difference between the rationalist and the poet is very *a propos* because he speaks about the poet trying to get his head into the heavens while the rationalist tries to get the heavens into his head.

Chesterton wants to show that the childlike approach to history would provide the truer framework for understanding the principles of the subject. For him, one of the principles of the subject is that history does not unfold from premises such as those from which a science would unfold. History can only be known with the degree of certainty that the subject matter allows. And since the subject matter is the story of mankind, it would best be understood by looking at the individual stories in the light of what our common sense tells us about human nature. The more deeply we understand human nature, the more light we will bring to bear on our imaginative replaying of the stories that make up human history.

Chesterton also shows the strategic role perception can play:

> Now the first fact is that the most simple people have the most subtle ideas. Everybody ought to know that, for everybody has been a child. Ignorant as a child is, he knows more than he can say and feels not only atmospheres but fine shades[12]

In this quote, Chesterton shows how intuition is just as important as discursive logical reasoning. Children intuit things, and only later learn to give the logical outline that supports what they know immediately. Truth can be known through the mediation of syllogisms, or it can be known without any mediating forms. This is the type of knowledge that poetry and literature give. They form pictures for the imagination to look at and rely on the human nature of the reader to draw the necessary conclusions. This sort of understanding can be called intuition or common sense, but it is common because it springs from the nature that all humans share.

Chesterton gives another example of this intuitive ability common to all human nature when he speaks about the human yearning for simplicity over complexity:

> ... the ancient instinct and humour of humanity have always told ... that the conventions of complex cities were less really healthy and happy than the customs of the countryside ... there is a real if only a recurrent yearning for that sort of simplicity; and there is never that sort of yearning for that sort of complexity.[13]

Here he points out that the common man instinctively seeks out the world uncluttered by the artifacts of mankind because it is more simple and consequently a more productive path toward health and happiness. This would imply that there is a congruence between man's happiness and the order of things that comes directly from the hand of God. This notion correlates with Chesterton's emphasis on locality as a pivotal influence on the course of history.

The particular topography of a locality influences the customs and happiness of a particular people, and since it is so essential to their well-being, it becomes an ever more important and closely-held element in their collective life. The temper and character of the Welshman differs from the temper and character of the Yorkshire man in no small measure because their local loves are fed by different kinds of beauty and natural harmonies.

In his biography of George Bernard Shaw, Chesterton points out the following:

> But among these, G.B.S. (these turnings of skepticism against the skeptics), there was one which has figured largely in his life; the most amusing and perhaps the most salutary of all these reactions. The "progressive" world being in revolt against religion had naturally felt itself allied to science; and against the authority of priests it would perpetually hurl the authority of scientific men. Shaw gazed for a few moments at this new authority, the veiled god of Huxley and Tyndall, and then with the greatest placidity and precision kicked it in the stomach. He declared to the astounded progressives around him that physical science was a mystical fake like sacerdotalism; that scientists, like priests, spoke with authority because they could not speak with proof or reason; that the very wonders of science were mostly lies, like the wonders of religion. 'When astronomers tell me,' he says somewhere, 'that a star is so far off that its light takes a thousand years to reach us, the magnitude of the lie seems to me inartistic.[14]

When he speaks about George Bernard Shaw's skepticism being directed equally against science and religion, Chesterton applauds Shaw's recognition that science rests on articles of faith just as religion does. However, Shaw shows a weakness in his thought in not being able to accept anything without proof, meaning a proof that is narrowly understood. He does not adhere to Aristotle's famous declaration that a thing can be known only to the degree that the subject matter allows.

Shaw's hardheaded rationalism makes the multi-dimensional character of reality less available to him because he feels discomfort in the presence of the paradoxical and dialectical elements in reality. Nevertheless, Chesterton admired Shaw's Celtic wit and delight in puncturing the solemn pronouncements of other rationalists. This quality in Shaw makes him a sort of Irish Mark Twain, but Shaw insists on trying to fit everything he encounters into a box that is too narrow to contain the paradoxical structures that comprise reality. In this sense, he is the opposite of Chesterton's poet who tries to get his head into the Heavens and fits instead Chesterton's description of the rationalist who tries to get the Heavens into his head.

When it comes to understanding patriotism, Shaw's outlook incapacitates him. The love of a local spot is something that Shaw would dismiss in favor of the love of humanity. The common man has affection for the place where he grows up, the beauties that are familiar to him, the accents that are pleasant to his ear, and will try accordingly to defend his local spot against attacks from without. Shaw would see this as petty and parochial and of little significance. He would be more at home with the cosmopolitan who easily moves from one locality to another but has no deep feeling or allegiance to any particular place.

Chesterton would point out that a world full of cosmopolitans would be a world that remained undeveloped, if only because no one would have sufficient motivation—read love—to invest the effort required to make any particular locality flower. The paradox is that only the world in which localities are loved can foster the kind of open-minded patriotism that affirms the localities of others. In other words, because a person has a place to call home, he or she can readily empathize with another's patriotic love.

Chesterton goes on to identify other limitations in Shaw's outlook:

> This blindness to paradox everywhere perplexes his [Shaw's] outlook. He cannot understand marriage because he will not understand the paradox of marriage; that the woman is all the more the house for not being the head of it. He cannot understand patriotism, because he will not understand the paradox of patriotism; that one is all the more human for not merely loving humanity. He does not understand Christianity because he will not understand the paradox of Christianity; that we can only really understand all myths when we know that one of them is true.[15]

Shaw's lack of understanding for the paradox of childhood is another example of his inability to accept paradox. This failure to grasp childhood has implications on his ability to see things clearly, as when he dismisses the finding of astronomers because he doesn't understand them. The sophisticated, or pseudo-sophisticated intellectual arrogance is very uncharacteristic of children, who will generally accept the reality of things with reasonable explanation.

> Exactly what Shaw does not understand is the paradox; the unavoidable paradox of childhood. Although this child is much better than I, yet I must teach it. Although this being has much purer passions than I, yet I must control it. Although Tommy is quite right to rush towards a precipice, yet he must be stood in the corner for doing it. This contradiction is the only possible condition of having to do with children at all; anyone who talks about a child without feeling this paradox might just as well be talking about a merman.[16]

History is capable of producing progress as well as regression: There is no one-way street. Just as the life of individual human beings is meandering, so is the collective life of nations. There is a sense in which the present time of a people can emphasize one thing to the exclusion of all others and thereby become oppressive in the weight that it brings to bear on a culture. Chesterton seems to think that the trick is to try and get outside of your own time imaginatively, so that you can come to some clearer-sighted understanding of what is good as well as what is bad. This again implies that Chesterton is an essentialist in the sense that he has a standard of human nature by which something can be judged to be good or bad.

One of the consequences of Chesterton's being an essentialist is that his standard for understanding history is not linked to any particular nation so much as it is tied to a human nature that all nations have in common. The freedom that is an essential characteristic of human nature can be exercised to the benefit or detriment of the individual human being or group of human beings. The old distinctions of virtue and vice point out that the good human being is the result of many good choices, and the bad human being the result of bad choices. In this sense, Chesterton affirms that every man is a self-made man, and perhaps by extension, every nation is a self-made nation. Some nations seem to bring a childish quality to the exercise of their human freedom in that they abdicate it in favor of some centralized control or wish to lose it in a sort of irrational fervor.

Chesterton clarifies the point that the Dark Ages (as distinct from the Middle Ages) were a period when such choices were made:

> The fierce and childish vow of the lords to serve their lord "against all manner of folk" obviously comes from the real Dark Ages; no longer confused, even by the ignorant, with the Middle Ages. [17]

Perhaps this childish way of exercising freedom is as much the result of fear as it is arrogance. Chesterton was deeply suspicious of the "German temperament" that was manifest in Prussia with its militaristic schemes of domination. He often wrote against it either directly in works such as *The Barbarism of Berlin*, or indirectly in his evocation of Nordic nihilism in *The Ballad of the White Horse*. His reaction to such schemes of large-scale control was understandable on several grounds. For one thing, he was a human being reacting to an abridgement of his own personal freedom, a freedom that constituted an essential quality of his humanity. But he was also aware that, even on pragmatic grounds, attempts to spread a local culture in a manipulative and oppressive way were doomed to fail from attenuation:

> There is one deep defect in our extension of cosmopolitan and Imperial cultures. That is, that in most human things if you spread your butter far you spread it thin. But there is an odder fact yet: rooted in something dark and irrational in human nature. That is, that when you find your butter thin, you begin to spread it. And it is just when you find your ideas wearing thin in your own mind that you begin to spread them among your fellow-creatures. It is a paradox; but not my paradox.[18]

The energies of a culture can be exhausted if they are not consistently replenished by some vital source. The roots of the word culture are found in the Latin *cultus*, meaning both cultivation of the land and reverence for the gods. Spiritual customs are an intrinsic part of any vibrant culture. Writers as disparate as Christopher Dawson and Perry Miller have pointed out the deep religious foundations that underlie such energetic cultures. Newman—arguably one of the deepest thinkers Victorian England produced—consistently reiterated *ad fontes* as the key to revivifying the religious structure of establishment England. He wanted to encourage a renewed appreciation for the thinking of the Church fathers with an eye toward buttressing the crumbling foundations of English culture. He saw the Church fathers—both Latin and Greek—as the true spiritual spring from which English culture flowed. Chesterton draws the connection between waning strength in a culture's spiritual roots and the outward push of imperialism. Paradoxically, when strength is most needed at home it is projected outwardly in an attempt to dominate others.

Chesterton also pointed out that not everything contained in human nature is rational. His acknowledgement of the irrational forces in human history is coupled with an acknowledgement of something dark. Thus, we are led to the role of evil as an antagonist in the drama of human history. Indeed, Chesterton acknowledged the influence of the diabolical in his own life when he spoke of his youthful encounter with evil in his autobiography. This personal encounter would naturally be a part of his understanding and interpretation of the collective life of nations. In both cases, it is a matter of the exercise of human freedom.

Chesterton saw that in his own time the elite of his society were embracing cultures with foundations outside of Christianity at the same time that they were promoting the extension of the British empire. An emphasis on Orientalism was apparent in everything, from the designs of William Morris to linguistic mores ("pukka sahib") to Eastern elements of architecture in the Art Nouveau movement to the emergence of Spiritualism among the middle and upper classes. This era also witnessed the return to fashion of pre-Christian Celtic and Anglo-Saxon paganism, from flower fairies and druids in art and literature to quasi-religious neo-pagan sects.

The historical writing of the time took on a more outwardly scientific and rationalistic tone at the same time as the metaphysical underpinnings of religious belief were evaporating. Accordingly, H.G. Wells could write of positive progression of historical events toward an ever-more enlightened present while rejecting the old way of writing history that emphasized the picturesque detail.

Henry Thomas Buckle was one of the prominent historical rationalists of the early Victorian age who was of the opinion that history was not the result of the free will of men, but of the inevitable chain of cause and effect, similar to that which governed the material world. In the following passage, it is clear that Buckle was a rationalist of the same kind as H.G. Wells.

Rejecting the metaphysical doctrine of free-will, and the theological dogma of predestined events, we are driven to the conclusion that the actions of men, being determined solely by their antecedents, must have a character of uniformity, that is to say, must, under precisely the same circumstances, always issue in precisely the same results.[19]

Buckle thinks the only cause of historical change is the amount of acquired knowledge at any given time. For him, scientific progress is the driving force of history and not religion. Unlike Chesterton, Buckle dismisses the supernatural and sees man's progress and the changes of history as a function of the knowledge of each generation. In his book, *History of Civilization in England,* Buckle states:

In a great and comprehensive view, the changes in every civilised people are in their aggregate dependent solely on three things; first, on the amount of knowledge possessed by their ablest men; secondly, on the direction which that knowledge takes, that is to say, the sort of subjects to which it refers; thirdly, and above all, on the extent to which the knowledge is diffused and the freedom with which it pervades all classes of society.[20]

Another Victorian historian, W.E.H. Lecky, admired Buckle's attempts to see history as an organic whole and attempted to carry on the tradition established by Buckle. He was concerned with the larger picture as opposed to a series of biographies or individual events. He saw a nation in almost anthropomorphic terms. In his *Historical and Political Essays,* Lecky states the following:

A true and comprehensive history should be the life of a nation. It should describe it in its larger and more various aspects. It should be a study of causes and effects, of distant as well as proximate causes, and of the large, slow and permanent evolution of things.[21]

Lecky bears an interesting resemblance to Chesterton in his emphasis on the role of imagination in history. He was an Irishman with a great interest in the literature as well as the history of his own country. His literary interest led him to attach great importance to the influence of stories and legends on a nation's history. He comments on this influence in the following passage from his book:

Legends which have no firm historical basis are often of the highest historical value as reflecting the moral sentiments of their time. Nor do they merely reflect them. In some periods they contribute perhaps more than any other influence to mould and colour them and to give them an enduring strength. The facts of history have been largely governed by its fictions. Great events often acquire their full power over the human mind only when they have passed through the transfiguring medium of the imagination, and men as they were supposed to be have even sometimes exercised a wider influence than men as they actually were. Ideals ultimately rule the world, and each before it loses its ascendancy bequeaths some moral truth as an abiding legacy to the human race. [22]

Like Lecky, the Victorian historian J.R. Green stressed the importance of seeing the whole rather than individual parts in the study of history. However, Green possessed an additional talent for imaginative re-creation of the past rather than the simple recounting of events. As the eminent British historian G.P. Gooch wrote in 1913, "He (Green) possessed a rare power of seizing the features of scenery and their effect on historical development."[23] This imaginative power is evident in the following excerpt from Green's *A Short History of the English People*.

> To all outer seeming Wales had in the thirteenth century become utterly barbarous. Stripped of every vestige of the older Roman civilization by ages of bitter warfare, of civil strife, of estrangement from the general culture of Christendom, the unconquered Britons had sunk into a mass of savage herdsmen, clad in the skins and fed by the milk of the cattle they tended, faithless, greedy, and revengeful, retaining no higher political organization than that of the clan, broken by ruthless feuds, united only in battle or in raid against the stranger. But in the heart of the wild people there still lingered a spark of the poetic fire which had nerved it four hundred years before, through Aneurin and Llywarch Hen, to its struggles with the Saxons. At the hour of its lowest degradation the silence of Wales was suddenly broken by a crowd of singers. The new poetry of the twelfth century burst forth, not from one bard or another, but from the nation at large.[24]

Green emphasized the importance of the land and the scenery as essential elements in the development of a people. He attempted to synthesize these elements in explaining why one people developed differently from another. He had great sympathy for the common people as distinct from the powerful groups in the church and state. This sympathy led him to delineate the development of specific localities and pay close attention to humble details while simultaneously trying to present an integrated picture of a nation's history. This aspect of Green's presentation of history can be seen in the following passage:

> At the close of the thirteenth century . . . all the more important English towns had secured the right of justice in their own borough-courts, of self-government, and of self-taxation, and their liberties and charters served as models and incentives to the smaller communities which were

struggling into life. During the progress of this outer revolution, the inner life of the English town was in the same quiet and hardly conscious way developing itself from the common form of the life around it into a form especially its own. Within as without the ditch or stockade which formed the first boundary of the borough, land was from the first the test of freedom, and the possession of land was what constituted the townsman. [25]

Another nineteenth century historian, J.A. Froude, differed from Buckle and his followers in that he was less of a materialist. Froude emphasized the pivotal influence of high ideals and aspirations to nobility in history, while respecting the mystery of human existence. However, he was no friend of the Catholic Church, seeing it as a force for oppression. As Gooch wrote, "The main occupation of his life was to combat the Roman Church." [26]

Froude stressed the importance of the great individuals in history. In his *Short Studies on Great Subjects*, he has the following to say:

> The address of history is less to the understanding than to the higher emotions. We learn in it to sympathize with what is great and good; we learn to hate what is base. In the anomalies of fortune we feel the mystery of our mortal existence; and in the companionship of the illustrious natures who have shaped the fortunes of the world, we escape from the littleness which clings to the round of common life, and our minds are tuned in a higher and nobler key.[27]

Froude was convinced of the dramatic element in history as evidenced by the struggles of great individuals to influence the course of events. He differs from Green to some degree in his stronger emphasis on the outstanding figures in history rather than the common people. This aspect of Froude's historical theory is stated in the following excerpt:

> For history to be written with the complete form of a drama, doubtless is impossible: but there are periods, and these the periods, for the most part, of greatest interest to mankind, the history of which may be so written that the actors shall reveal their characters in their own words; where mind can be seen matched against mind, and the great passions of the epoch not simply be described as existing, but be exhibited at their white heat in the souls and hearts possessed by them. [28]

Combining Green's interest in the common people with a strong antipathy for Buckle's rationalism was the Catholic historian, Lord Acton. Like Chesterton, Acton was profoundly convinced of the importance of religion in human affairs, and he was skeptical of attempts by small groups to exert power over the many. His departure from Buckle in a metaphysical understanding of reality was summarized in his statement that, "History compels us to fasten on abiding issues, and rescues us from the temporary and transient." [29]

Acton was convinced of an abiding spiritual presence in human affairs that made nature and form more important in history than mere accidental change. He saw modern history as the outcome of the interplay between power and the opposition to being dominated. Acton's liberalism also stressed the rights of smaller groups of people to be free from the constantly expanding power of majorities. As he said, "The first of human concerns is religion, and it is the salient feature of the modern centuries." [30]

The religious dispositions of a people frame their attitude toward human persons and provide the impetus for resistance to power that, unchecked, would expand ceaselessly. Acton saw this interplay between power and human freedom as the source of the drama of modern history. He described this phenomena in the following statement, "This law of the modern world, that power tends to expand indefinitely, and will transcend all barriers, abroad and at home, until met by superior forces, produces the rhythmic movement of History."[31]

The obvious parallel of Acton's philosophy with Chesterton's historical thinking is the emphasis on spiritual forces in history combined with a profound distrust of concentrated power. Nevertheless, they were in the minority as the impact of empiricism and Enlightenment ideals gained influence in historical circles of the time. Despite their differences of emphasis and imaginative power, for varying reasons Buckle, Froude, Green and Lecky shared a common distrust of spiritual considerations with a consequent tendency toward rationalism.

In the Victorian age, the colorful actions of persons who manifested virtue and vice—the type of history exemplified by Herodotus or Plutarch or even Charles Dickens' *Child's History of England*—were giving way to a more abstracted and scientific history. Von Ranke's dictum that history should deal only with facts made the German historians the model of historical scholarship to be imitated, even if indirectly, by the English. Chesterton saw that this new emulation of a more scientific history, while it may have had the advantage of a closer scrutiny of original documents, could nevertheless easily suffer from a blindness to the importance of non-empirical elements.

Chesterton also saw that the recording of factual detail was important for establishing what could be known about the past. But he was completely unwilling to dispense with the element of the intuitive and the artistic in understanding history. He believed that history could not be fully understood without recourse to one's own everyday experience of human nature as well as the imaginative element of picturesque details. It would be one thing to gather a hundred detailed facts and leave them open to interpretation, but quite another to impose a conclusion onto the facts that tried to fit them into a world view that was very narrow. The narrower the worldview, the fewer interpretations would be available to understand the many facts. Ideological historians in the twentieth century have shown this very aptitude for marshalling a large quantity of facts only to diminish their significance by forcing the facts into a preconceived mold.

By contrast, Chesterton had great faith in the average man's ability to be given a picturesque story from history and then to draw a true conclusion as to its meaning if his vision was not narrowed by rigid ideological constraints. Chesterton detected a trend in contemporary histories that eschewed the picturesque detail in favor of revisionist accounts. This trend was provoked more by a desire to tidy up inconsistencies that did not fit a pre-conceived idea rather than to at least partially portray some of the messy and paradoxical stories that comprise human history. He explained these different approaches in the following passage from the chapter "On the Writing of History" from his book, *Generally Speaking*:

> The early Victorian writer put in the picturesque detail and gave no explanation of it. The late Victorian writer took out the picturesque detail and gave no substitute for it.... The new histories were quite as unreliable as the old histories. The only difference was that the new histories were not only unreliable, but unreadable.[32]

Chesterton explains that: " ... the picturesque ... is a perfectly natural instinct of man for what is memorable." [33]

A concrete example of these two different approaches to historical analysis can be found in the contrasting perspectives of Chesterton and Gerald Bullett. Bullett was a contemporary of his who also wrote an early biography of him. He stated that Chesterton had room for the inexplicable and mysterious elements in history. However, Bullett's own agnosticism prevented him from including anything outside the natural as an explanation for historical fact:

> I am prepared to believe, let us say, that prodigies of healing, unfathomable by medical science have occurred and do occur. Mr. Chesterton also believes this. What divides us is not the historical fact but the philosophical inference to be drawn from that fact. I believe that these things are supernatural only in the sense that they are beyond our knowledge of nature: he believes that they are (as he has said) willful as well as wonderful, the work of a magician acting upon the world from outside it.... I myself, the most ordinary of agnostics, refuse to accept (that). [34]

Bullett sees the supernatural as only the natural that has yet to be fully understood by man. For him, the supernatural is a matter of cognition, and not something completely different in kind. Chesterton saw that the supernatural differed from the natural in both degree and kind.

Furthermore, Chesterton believed that man is a true secondary cause. Although when it came to the question of man's meaning, the full explanation could not be found without recourse to something transcendent. Man's freedom is a real freedom and not a caricature because his nature is a real seat of causality. The will that Chesterton saw working prior to man's will was not so much an interference as an invitation. He maintained that the world and nature are the result of a choice that precedes man's will. However, his freedom is nonetheless real and stands as an opportunity to participate in the will that precedes his own.

In a sense, Bullett's understanding of nature has less explanatory power than does Chesterton's because Bullett's agnosticism leaves many facts uncovered. Chesterton realized that to say that things have natures is the same as to say that things are the result of a free choice, and that that free choice necessarily precedes the existence of the thing.

The specificity of created entities also accounts for the importance of the picturesque in Chesterton's philosophy of history. Chesterton can never say enough about the concrete, pictoral details of an historical occurrence because this is how he comes closest to opening up the meaning of an event.

Responding to H.G. Wells's rejection of this manner of writing history as well as his dismissal of ritual as a holdover from a less-enlightened age, Chesterton wrote the following in a 1913 letter to an admirer, Bertram Hyde:

> About ritual itself I think the truest thing was said by Yeats the poet, certainly not a Catholic or even a Christian; that ceremony goes with innocence. Children are not ashamed of dressing-up, nor great poets at great periods, as when Petrarch wore the laurel. Our world does feel something of what Wells says, because our world is as nervous and irritable as Wells himself. But I think the children and the poets are more permanent. [35]

Chesterton points out the connection between an appreciation for the picturesque and a childlike spirit. When someone believes in something, he is not against colorful or external display to show that belief. For instance, soldiers wear their uniforms and medals; priests wear their cassocks; and high officials of state and magistrates wear their robes. Anyone who represents something greater than himself has the capacity to engage in ceremony and costume. Chesterton points out that the poet is a perfect example of one who enters fully into something that is not himself, and therefore is capable of dressing up without any self-consciousness. The lack of self-consciousness of children makes them have an affinity with the soldier, cleric or monarch because they, like these, have a strong desire to take full part in the world around them and forget themselves.

This connection between ceremony and innocence highlights a question of identity, because in each case cited above, a person identifies himself with something that transcends him, whether God or the State or the Law. Chesterton saw that the ability to identify oneself imaginatively with the various actors of the past was the best chance to understand history. Here again we see the reasons behind his emphasis on the legendary as a way of distilling the essential spirit of historical periods and events.

Chesterton's artistic talent and poetic temperament made him particularly suited to identify in this way with the historical past. He saw how his contemporaries would frame their approach to understanding history based not on an attempt to identify themselves with the past, so much as seeing history as a fulfillment of a need that presently concerned them. For example, H.G. Wells, who had no belief in a transcendent meaning for history, looked to his own country as a source of meaning instead. In this sense, he was a good example of the kind of patriotism that Chesterton saw would be destructive, namely one that would be a substitute for religion.

Wells' socialism manifested a distrust of individual persons and their ability to construct an orderly state without the help of an over-arching control. His patriotism was a faith in the British Empire that replaced his country's older faith in God. Chesterton comments on these characteristics of Wells in the following excerpt from his autobiography:

> Mr. Wells is not really a pacifist any more than a militarist; but the only sort of war he thinks right is the only sort of war I think wrong. Anyhow, broadly speaking, it is a complete mistake to suppose that the rebels who denounced Church and Chapel were those who denounced Empire and Army. The divisions cut across; but they were cut mainly the other way. A fighting Pro-Boer like MacGregor was in as much of a minority among atheists as among artists; even in Bedford Park. I soon discovered that, when I emerged into the larger world of artists and literary men.... The truth is that for most men about this time Imperialism, or at least patriotism, was a substitute for religion. Men believed in the British Empire precisely because they had nothing else to believe in. [36]

Chesterton's philosophy of history and emphasis on locality was greatly influenced by his much-admired predecessor, William Cobbett. Cobbett was a lover of the local, rural character of England, and he was saddened to see that the English farmers and yeomen were losing the power to support themselves. He was born in the mid-eighteenth century, and witnessed the encroachments of the Industrial Revolution. But Cobbett also looked back to the earlier encroachments of the newly-enriched Bourgeoisie that had emerged from the English Reformation.

Cobbett placed a great deal of store in being in contact with nature. He thought that a lack of direct experience with one's natural surroundings would make a person less human. He conveyed this idea in his books, particularly in *Rural Rides*. Chesterton admired Cobbett not for his great systematic philosophy, but for his large interior life through which he understood those things that are quintessentially English.

> All the time he (Cobbett) wandered on the bare baked prairies under that hard white light of the western skies, he had remembered the high green fields of his father's farm and the clouds and the comfort of the rain. For him even more than for Nelson, and in another sense, there was something united and almost interchangeable in the three terms of England, home, and beauty. [37]

Chesterton thought that Cobbett was an original man in the sense that he did not automatically take another person's view as the truth. Rather, he looked at the world and had enough confidence in his understanding to form his own opinions. Cobbett's opinions were formed more by direct experience than by copying the opinions of other people. He typified the rural English in that he grew up believing what his senses told him, since rural people live much closer to concrete realities than those in the stratified urban environment. This aspect of Cobbett's personality resonated with Chesterton the journalist who, as was discussed in chapter one, viewed history more from the vantage point of concrete realities and common sense than the theoretical abstractions of an ideology.

> He (Cobbett) was not a scientific man or in the orderly and conscious sense even a philosophical man. But he was, by this rather determining test, a great man. He was large enough to be lonely. He had more inside him than he could easily find satisfied outside him. He meant more by what he said even than the other men who said it. He was one of the rare men to whom the truisms are truths. This union of different things in his thoughts was not sufficiently thought out; but it was a union. It was not a compromise; it was a man. That is what is meant by saying that he was also a great man. There was something in him that the world had not taught him; even if it was too vast and vague for him to teach it to the world. [38]

Cobbett did not grow tired of contemplating simple things. When Chesterton said that he was one of those rare men to whom truisms are truths he meant that he had the unusual capacity to see the value of what many others would only consider commonplace.

I believe that there is something important in this context about how things that are local and familiar can easily become unnoticed and eventually invisible, and therefore not be valued. Chesterton was fond of saying that when you had looked at something for the twentieth time, you were really in danger of finally seeing it. The singular quality of Cobbett was that he did look at things and did talk about what he could see. He had the unusual boldness of not being swayed by what others would say was there, but insisted on identifying what he saw was there. This quality is often found in those who are living apart from great centers of media and opinion-forming organizations that exercise great persuasive influence over large numbers of people. As Chesterton wrote:

> This great delusion of the prior claim of printed matter, as something anterior to experience and capable of contradicting it, is the main weakness of modern urban society.[39]

Chesterton found several important kindred ideas in Cobbett's life as well. Chief among them was Cobbett's familiarity with the ordinary, concrete realities of local life and his ability to see them as beautiful, instead of pedestrian or ugly. Like Chesterton, Cobbett also fought against any forces that sought to control and subjugate these local beauties for individual satisfaction. For instance, William Cecil's Elizabethan police state exerted an efficient control that did nothing to encourage any such local loves. As such, both Cobbett and Chesterton found the Reformation to be the remote ancestor of the standardization found in industrial England.

Like Chesterton, Cobbett believed that a patriot could wind up opposing his own government. This seeming contradiction is made possible by an understanding of patriotism that does not place the state as the focus of loyalty or love, but sees it as a servant of those things worthy of love in any locality. Among these would be the encouragement of human freedom; the cultivation of the potential of the land; and artistic productions made possible by local conditions . . . all of which require a certain clarity of thought to recognize and appreciate.

In this respect, Chesterton the artist found much in common with Cobbett the clear-sighted farmer. Both looked at things until they saw them. By different roads, they came to the same destination that Chantal Millon-Delsol would later extol in her writings on subsidiarity, namely, that the most important function of the state is the historical one ensuring its non-interference in human flourishing.

Another predecessor of Chesterton's who had a profound influence on him was Sir Walter Scott. Writing in the decades preceding the Victorian era, Scott was a pioneer explorer of local historical lore and a lover of the concrete, picturesque details of the past. In this respect, it is immediately clear that Chesterton would find in Scott a vision of history sympathetic to his own.

The first noteworthy fact was that Scott was a writer of romances. His stories are about adventures in the sense that they involve the unexpected twists and turns that occur during a quest. In addition, they draw on the vivid details of local color that give life to a particular place and period in history. Scott was especially adept at describing in detail the material elements that give weight and texture to a romantic narrative.

The well-known characters Wamba, Cedric and Bois Gilbert all take on a vibrant life through Scott's ability to describe in detail the clothing, tools, and physical surroundings that fill the story. As adept as Scott was at evoking the fine material details of historical periods, he was even more alert to the depiction of situations that provoke a judgment of character. An example would be the scene of the contest between Bois Gilbert and Ivanhoe while Rebecca's fate hangs in the balance.

Chesterton is quick to appreciate Scott's ability in depicting concrete situations that capture a period as it unfolds. Chesterton describes this talent in one of his essays on Walter Scott:

> In estimating, therefore, the ground of Scott's pre-eminence in romance we must absolutely rid ourselves of the notion that romance or adventure are merely materialistic things involved in the tangle of a plot or the multiplicity of drawn swords. We must remember that it is, like tragedy or farce, a state of the soul evoked in us by the sight of certain places or the contemplation of certain human crises, by a stream rushing under a heavy and covered wooden bridge, or by a man plunging a knife or sword into tough timber. In the selection of these situations which catch the spirit of romance as in a net, Scott has never been equaled or even approached.[40]

For Chesterton, the spirit of romance involves the evocation of picturesque details, while at the same time combining these details with human crises to highlight the uniqueness of a particular historical period. With regard to any historical period, there is always something in common with every other historical epoch because the participants are human beings and, as such, they share a common human nature with other human beings in other historical eras. This shared nature is what makes it possible for the readers of history to identify with and consequently understand more fully the events that have taken place. Where Scott excelled was in his ability to give the multiplicity of details that conveyed the local qualities in such a manner as to bring them to life for the reader.

Unlike some critics of Scott, Chesterton admired his attention to the apparel of his characters. This delight in the material aspects bespoke of the love for his subject that Scott brought to his work. Herein lies a key to Scott's success as a historical novelist: to love something is to seek to identify oneself with it. Scott loved the historical details of a period for their own sake. He had an admiration for the different manners, dress, weapons and customs of people who lived in the past. Also, he wanted to know as much as possible about the details in order to bring to life what he admired.

Chesterton aligns this kind of love with a childlike spirit:

> . . . one of the charges most commonly brought against Scott, particularly in his own day—the charge of a fanciful and monotonous

insistence upon the details of armour and costume. The critic in the Edinburgh Review said indignantly that he could tolerate a somewhat detailed description of the apparel of Marmion, but when it came to an equally detailed account of the apparel of his pages and yeomen the mind could bear it no longer. The only thing to be said about that critic is that he had never been a little boy. . . . Like a child, he (Scott) loved weapons with a manual materialistic love, as one loves the softness of fur or the coolness of marble. One of the profound philosophical truths which are almost confined to infants is this love of things, not for their use or origin, but for their own inherent characteristics. . . . So it was with Scott, who had so much of the child in him.[41]

Chesterton's great regard for Scott's ability to depict highly-detailed scenes specific to a locality has implications for the broad appeal that Scott exercised over other writers of historical romance. In this area, Chesterton focuses on the paradox that brings together the universality of human nature and the only stage on which human nature can unfold, namely the local one.

Scott's concentration on the details of a historical scene built up a vivid national picture of Scotland and England. He displayed these national images in such an evocative way, while capturing the personalities unique to particular periods, that writers of different nationalities were able to find inspiration from him for their own literary works. In his essay, "On Sir Walter Scott", Chesterton credits Scott with not only the creation of a Scottish national literature, but indirectly, with a European literature as well:

. . . every writer who is really universal is also national; but Scott was not merely national, but very universal. Continental poets, like Goethe and Victor Hugo, would hardly have been themselves without Scott. . . . Scott made Scottish Romances, but he made European Romance.[42]

Scott demonstrated a love for the romance and adventure to be found in one's local milieu, as well as an appreciation for the concrete material aspects of history. Chesterton particularly prized both of these qualities in him.

Scott also had an ability to go beyond the unexpected events and the concrete material details of history and draw out the spiritual realities that infused a particular period, giving it life and purpose. Chesterton would argue that without the ability to marshal a large number of concrete physical details, and without the ability to depict dramatic scenes involving the interplay of human personalities, a writer of historical romance would be unable to arrive at an understanding of the ideas and ideals which motivate and inspire a given group of people in history. Therefore, it is precisely through Scott's great regard for local details and colors that he is able to identify with and present scenes of distinctive historical quality.

With his distinctive historical sense, Scott was then able to draw out the spirit that was valued and promoted, and which gave rise to the visible manifestations and human confrontations that comprised the historical period. As Chesterton observed:

> One thing he did find in the past, not yet quite destroyed in the present, and it was his chief inspiration . . . he had extracted from his feudal traditions something on which his spirit truly fed; something without which the modern world is starving. He found the idea of Honour, which is the true energy in all militant eloquence. That a man should defend the dignity of his family, of his farm, of his lawful rank under that King, even of his mere name, of something at least that was larger than himself—this was the fire that Scott found still burning out of fourteenth-century feudalism and expressed in eighteenth-century oratory. Of all moral ideals it is the most neglected and misunderstood today. [43]

What Chesterton perceived as Scott's strength, namely the ability to draw out the spirit of a particular historical period, was in fact one of Chesterton's own great abilities as well. Unlike Wells, who saw history in a linear and rationalist outline, Chesterton made allowances for the real freedom of human nature. The local patriotism of Cobbett reinforced Chesterton's sense of the importance of the love of familiar things. But Chesterton departed from Cobbett in his largeness of understanding and sympathy for the legitimate patriotism of other peoples. Belloc's views on the importance of private property and the threat of the overwhelming state had a great influence on Chesterton's historical vision. In contrast to Belloc, however, Chesterton was inclined to an artistic rendering of his ideas rather than a polemical depiction.

Shaw's atheism and socialism served as a catalyst for Chesterton's development of his own ideas. It is clear that Chesterton borrowed ideas from some of these contemporaries and received encouragement and corroboration for others. But he was nonetheless the "strong poet" whom Bloom speaks of, in that he was able to make use of the ideas of his contemporaries and predecessors without being subsumed into their thought. Instead, he developed his original conceptions of the meaning of history; conceptions fed by his own artistic outlook, a childlike delight in material reality, and a penetrating intelligence that would not be satisfied with an oversimplification of the complexities and the paradoxes that he found imbedded in the nature of reality.

3 The Critical Lens

In the chapter entitled "History versus the Historians" in his book *Lunacy and Letters,* Chesterton returns to his theme that literary approaches to history often do more to bring the past to life than purely formal historical works. This is because the literary writer is attempting to describe individualized human beings while the historian is constrained by the more rudimentary factual material at his disposal.

> Most modern notions of the earlier and better Middle Ages are drawn either from historians or from novels. The novels are very much the more reliable of the two. The novelist has at least to try to describe human beings; which the historian often does not attempt. [1]

Chesterton points out the importance of the descriptive in any attempt to recreate the past. Since the novel depicts a world peopled with characters who speak, eat, and live in a specific place, it is more likely to capture the imagination of the reader than a lifeless recounting of facts. To be a good historical novelist of this type would require not only a sharp eye for the details of human life, but also a strong sympathy with many varied human types. Chesterton recognized in Geoffrey Chaucer just such a sympathetic and sharp-eyed observer of the Middle Ages. He looked to Chaucer for a vibrant historical picture of his time precisely because of these qualities. Chesterton himself exhibited Chaucerian qualities to a great degree. Noel O'Donoghue comments on Chesterton's portrayal of the past:

> [Chesterton was] an artist, a maker of pictures, a supreme master in the invention of image and the uses of imagination: simile, metaphor, contrast, hyperbole, irony, exaggeration.[2]

Chesterton saw in Chaucer a man who actually lived during the historical period about which he wrote, and valued his testimony even more than the muted testimony of court records, land deeds and royal proceedings. Chaucer's testimony was motivated by a real affection for the characters he described. Above all, Chaucer was a poet of the local. In *The Canterbury*

Tales, he narrows his vision to a small swath of land in southern England peopled by characters whose idiosyncrasies marked them as distinctive persons. Chaucer gives a picture of everyday life that is better than any other English writer of the time.

Chesterton comments in *Lunacy and Letters* on the scarcity of such testimony and its historical importance:

> But there is another humble class of men who might be allowed to tell us something about the Middle Ages. I mean the men who lived in the Middle Ages. There are in existence medieval memoirs which are nearly as amusing as Pepys, and much more truthful. In England, they are almost entirely unknown. But I am very glad to find that the Chronicles of Joinville and the Chronicles of Villehardouin have been translated into excellent English.... Let anyone open Joinville's rambling story, and he will find the Middle Ages of Macaulay and Rossetti and Dickens and Miss Jane Porter fall from him like a cumbrous cloak. He will find himself among men as human and sensible as himself, a little more brave and much more convinced of their first principles.... The reader will find it impossible not to respect the man; his lumbering punctiliousness about truth ... his perpetual and generous praise of others in battle; his rooted affections and simple pride in the affection of others for him; his slight touchiness about his dignity as a gentlemen.[3]

The characters in Chaucer's *Canterbury Tales* are contemporaries of one another who share the same climate and are familiar with the same customs. This commonality is a crucial characteristic of a nation. It seems that Chesterton links together Chaucer's depiction of the local characters of Canterbury with the fledgling national character of the English. For Chesterton, a key role of Chaucer the writer is to memorialize these characteristic traits of the local types and thus present to the English people a mirror in which their particular qualities are presented. Such a reflection would allow a people to develop a sense of identity in which they are shown to be different from other groups. Therefore, an important function of a country's literature is to provide the self-knowledge and cohesive self-portrait that make a nation recognizable.

In his book on Chaucer, Chesterton speaks about the creative quality of Chaucer's literary work:

> The medieval word for a Poet was a Maker, which indeed is the original meaning of a Poet. It is one of the points, more numerous than some suppose, in which Greek and medieval simplicity nearly touch. There was never a man who was more of a Maker than Chaucer. He made a national language; he came very near to making a nation. At least without him it would probably never have been either so fine a language or so great a nation. Shakespeare and Milton were the greatest sons of

their country; but Chaucer was the Father of his Country, rather in the style of George Washington. And apart from that, he made something that has altered all Europe more than the Newspaper: the Novel.[4]

In the citation above Chesterton shows Chaucer's writing to be creative in more than one sense. He is making a work of art that has value as something beautiful in its own right and he is also making explicit the dimly perceived qualities of a national character. These qualities would remain vague and undelineated without the perceptive eye and expressive talent of Chaucer the writer.

In painting the detailed picture of characteristically English people, Chaucer carefully focused on colorful details such as the clever worldliness of the Wife of Bath and the coarse manners of the Miller. This focus on details brings the characters to life and highlights the relationship between the local and the universal. This paradoxical relationship is a result of an understanding of human nature that Chaucer drank in through the chief influences of his age, namely the Catholic faith and the heritage of Greek and Roman culture.

In an essay entitled "On Mr. Geoffrey Chaucer", Chesterton details this connection between the local and the universal:

> Chaucer was wide enough to be narrow; that is, he could bring a broad experience of life to the enjoyment of local or even accidental things. Now, it is the chief defect of the literature of today that it always talks as if local things could only be limiting, not to say strangling; and that anything like an accident could only be a jar. A Christmas dinner, as described by a modern minor poet, would almost certainly be a study in acute agony: the unendurable dullness of Uncle George, the cacophonous voice of Aunt Adelaide. But Chaucer, who sat down at the table with the Miller and the Pardoner, could have sat down to a Christmas dinner with the heaviest uncle or the shrillest aunt. He might have been amused at them, but he would never have been angered by them, and certainly he would never have insulted them in irritable little poems. And the reason was partly spiritual and partly practical; spiritual because he had, whatever his faults, a scheme of spiritual values in their right order, and knew that Christmas was more important than Uncle George's anecdotes; and practical because he had seen the great world of human beings, and knew that wherever a man wanders among men . . . he will find that the world largely consists of Uncle Georges.[5]

Chesterton further points out how Chaucer is an affable and even merry poet in his sympathy for his characters. Chaucer likes his characters even with their faults because he is broad minded enough to know that all human beings are flawed, and yet remain lovable despite the flaws. Influenced as he was by the fundamental Christian doctrine of original sin, Chaucer took for granted the weaknesses of his fellow men. His Christian sensibility affirmed the essential goodness of God's creatures and he was reaffirmed in this belief by the whole story of Christian redemption. Perhaps Chaucer's attitude could be profitably contrasted with writers of a more Calvinist cast whose influence prevailed in the England of Chesterton's time. The Calvinist emphasis on complete depravity and personal election would make it difficult for post-Reformation English writers to look at the world with the same merry, open attitude that Chaucer manifested in his writing. Chesterton is quick to tie together Chaucer's historical attitude with the prevailing philosophical and theological vision of his time.

In his book, *Chaucer*, Chesterton accentuates the sources of the author's worldview. Although never completely compatible with each other, the two forces he underscores were nevertheless the foundations for Chaucer's approach to understanding man:

> Perhaps the largest fact about the Middle Ages is that two forces worked and to some extent warred in that time. One was the mystical vision, or whatever we call it, which Catholics call the Faith; the other was the prodigious prestige of Pagan Antiquity. [6]

From Pagan antiquity, Chaucer received the seminal idea of a human nature. This idea was fundamental to his understanding of the element of consistency in human behavior despite the local differences. From Christianity, he received the idea of the person that built on the Greek concept of human nature and enriched it with the insights gained from Revelation.

The nature of man would help to explain why similarities are inevitable in human societies. The local influences would help to explain why there are also real differences, while the doctrine of man's creation in the image of God would explain further why he is to be valued wherever he is found. Chaucer's literary creation flows from a stream that is fed by these ancient sources and the resulting confluence made for a unique depiction of medieval man. Chesterton values Chaucer for the literary and, more pertinently, historical insight which he provides; an insight that is closer to the truth about the Middle Ages than any of Chaucer's intellectual descendents discerned. This appreciation is described in the following passage:

> The challenge of Chaucer is that he is our one medieval poet, for most moderns; and he flatly contradicts all that they mean by medieval. Aged and crabbed historians tell them that medievalism was only filth, fear, gloom, self-torture and torture of others. Even medievalist aesthetes tell them it was chiefly mystery, solemnity and care for the supernatural to the exclusion of the natural. Now Chaucer is obviously less like this than the poets after the Renaissance and

the Reformation. He is obviously more sane even than Shakespeare, more liberal than Milton; more tolerant than Pope; more humorous than Wordsworth, more social and at ease with men than Byron or even Shelley. [7]

The historians to whom Chesterton refers are found to be looking at the Middle Ages from the outside rather than the inside. These are the Whig historians who did so much to shape the historical attitudes of the Victorian period. They looked back at the epoch before the Reformation and saw it as synonymous with the abuses that the Reformation sought to correct. They failed to pay close attention to the widespread religious faith that made the abuses of the late Middle Ages possible. For instance, it was only because people believed in Catholicism that it was possible to sell indulgences. No one in Dickens' London would consider buying or selling indulgences because it would be considered unprofitable.

Chaucer's pilgrims are all going toward Canterbury because they believe in the miraculous powers of Becket's bones. Although their differences on a personal level may be quite striking, they hold a deep religious faith in common. The Victorian historians did not spend enough time considering the unifying character of such a widely held religious faith.

These historians also noted the deficiencies of medieval feudalism compared with the parliamentary democracy of modern times. They could not see that there was an element of freedom and initiative within the feudal system that allowed men to exercise their powers unhindered by the local nobility. Thus, both politically and religiously the Victorian historians found the Middle Ages to be lacking. Perhaps the most needed quality for such historians would have been a greater imaginative capacity to place themselves in the fourteenth century and observe the human pageant such as Chaucer described in *The Canterbury Tales*.

Ironically, a more imaginative understanding of Chaucer's time would allow for a fuller understanding of the very developments of Whig political history that colored the attitudes of Victorian historians. The local freedom enjoyed by medieval people advanced with the growth of the towns and the bourgeoisie and made parliamentary democracy a desirable development for the middle classes. In *A Short History of England*, Chesterton credits the local freedoms of feudal society for instilling a permanent desire for liberty in the English heart.

> The feudal units grew through the lively localism of the Dark Ages, when hills without roads shut in a valley like a garrison. Patriotism had to be parochial; for men had no country, but only countryside. In such cases the lord grew larger than the king; but it bred not only a local lordship but a kind of local liberty. And it would be very inadvisable to ignore the freer element in Feudalism in English history. For it is the one kind of freedom that the English have had and held. [8]

Chesterton again highlights the connection between localism and patriotism. The geographical qualities that separate one group of people from another provide an isolation that encourages similar experiences. These common experiences foster the development of a common identity, leading to local loyalties and patriotism. The land that sustained the local people was naturally an object of affection and, having given life to the local population, it would be natural for them to defend it with their own lives. The lord of the land became a lord through his feats of arms in defending the locality. His hold on the loyalty to the local people was proportionate to how well he organized their defense in time of need. For the most part, the people remained loyal because through him they were able to defend and sustain their terrain.

In banding together and organizing the defense of the terrain that sustained them, the countrymen of the Middle Ages were setting down the foundations for society. After defense would come affirmation expressed through common worship and celebration. These two are tied together because of the intrinsic connection between the goodness of the created order and the thanksgiving given to the Creator. This would often result in the building of a local church that came about from the large and small contributions of the lord and the people. One modern writer who examines this connection in detail is Josef Pieper. He underscores the essential relationship between the affirmation of the Divine Being and the goods of creation that takes place in any celebration or festival.[9]

The celebrations that marked the rhythm of communal life found their cause in thanksgiving to the Creator and commemoration of important dates in the history of the locality. Examples would be deliverance from an invader through their own hard fighting and the intercession of a patron saint, or the successful harvesting of a crop despite difficult weather conditions. The local religious bond was manifested in the form of parishes that provided the venue for both common worship and regular occasions for the people to meet and foster relationships.

As the countryside became more settled and people began to perform more specialized functions, it was also natural to form various guilds that provided regulations of the trades and exchange of knowledge of the crafts. In this way, what began as a sharing of a common local terrain grew into a multi-faceted exchange of the most valued human interests; work, religion, and festivity. The deep attachment of these human goods together with an attachment to the local land that nourished them explained the closely defended love that goes by the name of patriotism.

Chesterton points out that the state's approval of such multiple local flowerings came after they were fully in existence. These flourishing guilds, parishes and local festivals were not something given by the state, but rather they helped form the state and only asked its approval as an afterthought. In *A Short History of England*, Chesterton elaborates on the small local beginnings of the state:

The medievals not only had self-government, but their self-government was self-made. They did indeed, as the central powers of the national monarchies grew stronger, seek and procure the stamp of state approval; but it was approval of a popular fact already in existence. Men banded together in guilds and parishes long before Local Government Acts were dreamed of. Like charity, which was worked in the same way, their Home Rule began at home.... In modern constitutional countries there are practically no political institutions thus given by the people; all are received by the people. There is only one thing that stands in our midst, attenuated and threatened, but enthroned in some power like a ghost of the Middle Ages: the Trades Unions.[10]

Initiative-taking was a dominant characteristic of the medieval man who provided the foundation for this local self-government. The very origins of the noble families who comprised the local lordships came from those who took initiatives in feats of arms and organizing the local people into a system of vassals and loyal retainers. Perhaps this quality of planning was partially to rectify the lack of formal infrastructure in society that Chesterton alludes to when he speaks of the roadless Dark Ages. It certainly seems true that it was a time of building not only the structures of self-rule and religious life, but also the building of visible structures such as churches and halls that served as meeting places for communal activity and bore witness to the unity of the local people, if only because the cooperation of so many people was required to build them.

In *Eugenics and Other Evils,* Chesterton emphasizes that the medieval people succeeded above all in the art of architecture:

> For instance, the Middle Ages will simply puzzle us with their charities and cruelties, their asceticism and bright colours, unless we catch their general eagerness for building and planning, dividing this from that by walls and fences—the spirit that made architecture their most successful art.[11]

The monumental cathedrals that are found throughout England are mute testimony to the strong community life that pervaded even small localities. While the Yorkminster is a well-known example of a grand cathedral attached to an important town, the Salisbury cathedral holds its own as a beautiful example of the achievement of a smaller town.

The communal character of so much of the medieval man's activity stands in strong contrast to the individualism of the Victorian era. Chesterton points out in *The Victorian Age in Literature* that the novel is the natural art form to dominate in Victorian times because of its concern with individuals and their differences. The Middle Ages was concerned above all with those things that people held in common; their religion, their land, their buildings, and their customs. Perhaps most telling is the common sense that people shared regarding the essentials in life. Most people agreed on the basic assumptions underlying reality. This common sense allowed them to be able to argue with fruitfulness rather than futility. It also allowed a disparate group of people such as the Canterbury pilgrims to travel toward a common destination together without feeling repelled by each other.

In *Lunacy and Letters*, Chesterton gives the thirteenth century credit for being the age of common sense. He emphasizes the shared agreement on basic perceptions:

> If the eighteenth century was the Age of Reason, the thirteenth was the Age of Commonsense. When St. Louis said that extravagant dress was indeed sinful, but that men should dress well 'that their wives might the more easily love them', we can feel the age that is talking about facts, and not about fads.[12]

The practicality of St. Louis' remark is a good example of a simple wisdom to which the common man would readily assent and which became less apparent in later, more rationalistic times. Chesterton saw the Middle Ages as a time in which men may have outwardly given homage to their lords and kings, but on all the most important matters, they retained a belief in the dignity of each person as bearing the imprint of the Creator and worthy of respect.

One of the most fundamental truths held in common was the effect of original sin. The commoner would not be surprised to see the king doing penance for his sins any more than his closest neighbor. Henry II was publicly scourged after inciting the murder of Thomas Becket. In Chesterton's own age the spectacle of a leader, say, William Gladstone, doing public penance is hardly to be envisioned much less enacted.

In *What's Wrong With The World*, Chesterton aligns the Darwinian influence of his own time with a kind of progression from inequality to equality:

> The common conception among the dregs of Darwinian culture is that men have slowly worked their way out of inequality into a state of comparative equality. The truth is, I fancy, almost exactly the opposite. All men have normally and naturally begun with the idea of equality; they have only abandoned it late and reluctantly, and always for some material reason of detail. They have never naturally felt that one class of men was superior to another; they have always been driven to assume it through certain practical limitations of space and time.[13]

Chesterton credits the marked inequality of his age with an imposition of fads on the common people rather than the sort of common sense he attributes to St. Louis. The monarchy and nobility of the Middle Ages had been replaced with an oligarchy of the wealthy, comprised of an alliance between the remnants of the aristocracy and the newly-empowered middle classes. In Chesterton's view, this oligarchy exerted a more oppressive control over the mass of common people than any medieval power ever did. The common sense and assumptions that bound king and commoner together had been dispensed with in the age of reform and Enlightenment, leaving the localities of England more open to the self-interested maneuvers of the aristocracy and merchant class.

The influence of these latter even extended to the revisionist interpretation of history by contemporary writers. Chesterton thinks that the truth could be better realized by trying to see the past with a clear imagination uncluttered by the schoolbook history that expressed the sympathies and aversions of the oligarchs.

One critic sees Chesterton as attempting to rectify the damage done to the Middle Ages by the Victorian historians:

> Chesterton pays enormous attention to the Middle Ages. They have, he thinks, been rather badly dealt with by historians. Too much attention is, he contends, paid to the time of the Stuarts onwards. Chesterton asks us to contemplate history as we should if we never learnt it at school [14]

We have already seen how Chesterton prefers the novelistic interpretation of the past to the writings of many historians, because he sees the novelist trying to imaginatively describe human beings while the historians proceed from a rationalist perspective that values facts only narrowly understood.

In his monograph on Chaucer, Chesterton expends considerable energy sifting through the few facts that are known of Chaucer's life and dismissing some of the more elaborate historical conclusions drawn from them. He is satisfied to contemplate the simple and limited features that can be depicted of Chaucer based on these few facts. Chesterton seems to have an imaginative capacity to such a large degree that he is capable of putting himself in Chaucer's place and, knowing what he knows about his own human nature and that of others, reaches common sense conclusions based on the facts available. In this respect, he is like the twentieth-century historian Johan Huizinga, whose historical works depend largely on great intuitive powers as well as powers of imaginative expression.[15]

Another confirmation of this intuitive and imaginative quality of Chesterton's writing is found in the testimony of the Thomist, Etienne Gilson, who remarked that Chesterton's historical biography of Aquinas was the best account of the saint's life and work that he had ever seen. This is all the more remarkable given that, according to Chesterton's secretary, Dorothy Collins, he wrote the book on Thomas Aquinas with very little consultation of historical sources.[16]

Chesterton was at pains to make his reader see the contours of Chaucer the man and the age in which he lived. The emphasis is naturally on the verb to "see" because Chesterton is operating under the assumption that most people are blind to many of the most common and obvious truths as a result of routine ways of looking at the world. His famous advice that every man should break into his own house every once in a while to appreciate it fully is equally true of his approach to history. In his view, the poet will often succeed where the historian fails because the poet is by profession someone who breaks through the dull and routine way of seeing the world, and presents it with the splendor of its original form.

Chaucer is concerned with love in its manifold varieties in his *Canterbury Tales*. Chesterton appreciates Chaucer's ability to convey these attitudes in a way that synchronizes with human nature throughout all historical periods while showing the distinctive attributes of the era. In *Chaucer*, Chesterton notes that medieval people were able to distinguish between the paradoxes of love and the happiness to be found in it in a way that was easily recognizable by anyone. Their attitudes toward such a fundamental human concern are essential to a deeper understanding of the period in which they flourished. Chesterton intuitively understands that if one can grasp the attitude of a given people in a time period toward love or some similarly universal human concern, one could go a long way toward explaining many of the more peripheral details of their lives.

> . . . those who understand neither the fantastic nor the normal have pretended that all medieval men and women saw love and marriage merely as rivals to each other; accepted no marriage except as a dull duty; and enjoyed no love except as an illicit enjoyment. But this is all nonsense; not only to anybody who knows a little of human nature, but to anybody who knows even a little of medieval literature. The truisms remain true, however much fun people may get out of the paradoxes; the cynical paradoxes of satire, or the romantic paradoxes of adventure. A man imagines a happy marriage as a marriage of love; even if he makes fun of marriages that are without love, or feels sorry for lovers who are without marriage. That Chaucer was normal in this, as in nearly everything else, is abundantly proved by his own printed words. [17]

Here, Chesterton touches on the whole courtly love tradition that has been the source of so much critical literary commentary. Without judging the specific merits of any of these commentaries, Chesterton manages to point out the obvious human elements that would inform ideas of human love in a society permeated with Christianity.

Writers such as Andreas Capellanus might spill much ink on all the intricate rules that governed courtly flirtations and affairs, but such writing would ultimately have to be judged in the light of what was known about medieval man from other sources. These sources would include Chaucer's popular poetry and the understanding of human nature shown not only through the literary but also the philosophical works of the period. Because Chesterton is such a generalist and has a great interest in many aspects of life, he is more prone to correct and adjust his picture of a historical period with his highly developed common sense, as well as with his artistic sense and knowledge of individual character that was a fruit of liking so many different types of people.

Chesterton could discern the difference between a game played by the aristocracy extolling the glamour of adulterous love and the commonly accepted notion that monogamous marriage was the rule rather than the exception. Nevertheless, in this diversion of the ruling class he could see the faint outline of a tragedy that he would later analyze in his book, *The Superstition of Divorce*: "It is generally summarized by saying that the tragic element (in divorce) is the absence of love."[18] To a great degree, Chesterton had the quality of being able to see the small thing before it became large and obvious to everyone. This is a useful quality for the historian who is attempting to trace the pathways of ideas and customs as they exert lesser or greater influence upon the generations.

Another example of this quality can be found in Chesterton's writings on Chaucer, the man who, although he was the son of a vintner, was accepted into the elite circles of the king and his court. In this acceptance, he sees the beginning of a historical process that saw the middle classes first becoming useful to the aristocracy and then becoming their equals in power and wealth.[19] Although this process was in its early stages, Chesterton sees the task of the historian as that of a detective who notices the small features of a particular time and uses his common sense and knowledge of human nature to form a picture of what life was like. The task would then be to connect this picture with what life would become.

Chesterton sees Chaucer's overall historical contribution as the author who painted the most vivid pictures of individual characters, and described them with their follies and talents using the common sense understanding of human nature that was breathed by the average medieval person. Chaucer built his stories on the foundations of medieval logic and philosophy that were rooted in Aristotle and married to Christianity. He had a coherent view of the world that was broad and universal because it could include revelation as well as reason, and find them part of the same creation. This was in contrast to the experience of the Victorians who inherited a fragmented worldview from the Reformation and the narrower rationalism of the Enlightenment.

When Chesterton moves from criticism of medieval literature to criticism of the literature of his own age, he finds a strikingly different atmosphere; an atmosphere dominated by the philosophy of utilitarianism and the historical ideas of Whigs such as Macaulay. The utilitarianism of Bentham promoted the idea of the greatest good for the greatest number as a kind of mathematical optimization of human society. This philosophy fit in well with the faith in progress displayed by the Whig historians. Macauley and Bentham shared a common faith in the power of industrial wealth to make a nation great. Chesterton takes issue with the narrowness of what they considered to be great. He sees these foundational thinkers of the Victorian period to be men who had been severed from the broader and deeper foundations of English culture that he explored in his criticism of Chaucer. As a result, their influences provoked reaction among many of the sensitive artistic souls of their time. These latter were living off the richness and humanity of an English tradition that had its roots in the Middle Ages. For Chesterton, the irony was that, although the conscious formulae of the Victorian Age were narrow and impoverished, the unconscious tradition that still fed the common people was rich and humane.

In spite of this, Chesterton sees much to admire and praise in the Victorians. In his book, *Lunacy and Letters*, he goes beyond the dreary costume of the early Victorian gentlemen to see that they had an optimism about their future and wished to build something worthwhile, not merely looking back on the good that had been done before them.

> The early Victorian period, probably the finest that England has seen for a long time, is supposed to have been prosaic merely because it was ugly. The hats and trousers of Robert Browning and Lord Shaftsbury were indeed as hideous as their souls were beautiful; but they were not the only hideous generation, nor the most hideous. There were costumes in the Middle Ages, for instance—terrifying costumes with horned and towering head-dresses, enormous and curling shoes—which were quite as ugly, strictly speaking. . . . For the early Victorian age was, in its way, an age of faith, and of ugly clothes, like some of those medieval epochs. They believed themselves to be in a time of stir and promise; with them ambitions were poetic as well as memories. They brought poetry into politics.[20]

When Chesterton looks more closely at the optimistic goals of the early Victorians, however, he sees that some of their optimism was misplaced. They had put their faith in the commercial power of their country—a faith that seemed justified because of their blossoming industry and their network of maritime contacts. Nevertheless, this emphasis on commerce produced military conflicts in foreign countries and impoverished the lower classes at home.

Chesterton refers to this dilemma in *The Victorian Age in Literature*:

> The Victorian Age made one or two mistakes but they were really useful; that is, mistakes that were really mistaken. They thought that commerce outside a country must extend peace: it has certainly often extended war. They thought that commerce inside a country must certainly promote prosperity; it has largely promoted poverty. But for them these were experiments; for us they ought to be lessons. If we continue the capitalist use of the populace—if we continue the capitalist use of external arms, it will lie heavy on the living. The dishonor will not be on the dead.[21]

Looking back at the effects of the optimistic early Victorians, Chesterton considers them successful in having built a commercially powerful nation, but at the cost of a deadened spiritual life in the upper classes and a desperation in the lower classes. The upper echelons of society had largely ceased to take their religion seriously, the established church having become a place of privilege and comfort. The church also did not challenge the aristocracy to behave with anything more than decency. To Chesterton, writers such as Matthew Arnold appeared as apologists for the preservation of the established church who did not want it dismantled but nevertheless did not wish it to be truly Christian.[22]

Chesterton thought that Arnold was trying to practice a type of state religion: England and English culture were worthy of being preserved even though the ideals and influences which paved the way to its greatness were no longer being affirmed. The idea of the contract had replaced the medieval idea of the oath as a foundational principle in English social life.

In *The Superstition of Divorce*, Chesterton devotes an entire chapter to the notion of the vow. He sees this as a personal promise that united people on the social level in feudalism and on the personal level in marriage. It was a means whereby particular persons chose to tie their lives to a certain place and certain persons. As such, it was a limiting factor in the lives of everyone. By means of this limitation, the growth and development of local areas was made possible. Families were ordered on the stable basis of lifelong fidelity and the bonds of loyalty among various professions and military powers were intended to endure.

Chesterton places the Victorian contract in contrast to a society built on the vow or the oath. The contract is a utilitarian instrument that is directed toward mutual benefit and profit, which can be dispensed with when it is no longer useful to either party. The contract is not bound to the quality of loyalty to particular persons or places. As a result, it does not encourage the stabilization of local or even national bonds.

Chesterton was in favor of a culture that saw the human as creative rather than useful. A culture built on contracts subordinates the creativity of the person to the usefulness of the person relative to some goal—usually economic. A culture built on an understanding of human persons as creative places value on the ability of each person to establish bonds to a local place and people. Through the binding power of a promise, individuals would create something worthwhile for that specific place. This creation in its most common form would be a family, a profession or craft, or perhaps an association with the purpose of building a great work, such as a meeting house or a place of worship.

A society is to a large extent built to mirror the fundamental conception of man that it holds to be true. If persons are considered as means to an end, then the society tends to be ordered along the lines of whatever benefits can be achieved by organizing men for the profit of a minority. Those who are capable of controlling the resources, property, and means of production will tend to dominate. If man is viewed as fundamentally a creator, then the society would be structured accordingly so that his creative energies would be allowed to develop and bring works to completion. Such a society is founded on the notion that the person is an end unto him or herself, and not to be directed toward any other end.

Chesterton thinks that imperialism is the foreign policy of a society that is built on contracts rather than oaths. Imperialism attempts to subjugate and control other peoples and localities other than one's own using the population as pawns in a game that benefits the subjugators. The focus is taken off what is locally desirable and worthy of cultivation, and placed on something foreign.

The critic Patrick Braybrooke points out this anti-imperialism in Chesterton's work:

> For Chesterton, Imperialism is something that is both weak and perilous. It is really, he contends, a false idealism which tends to try and make people locally discontented, contented with pseudo visions of distant realms where the cities are of gold, where blue skies are never hidden by yellow fog. [23]

Imperialism would exert a destabilizing force on a country by directing the attention outward and toward an attempt to control cultures that are not fully understood nor appreciated. The kind of national pride and stubbornness inculcated by imperialist success would tend to make a people flee from their local problems in favor of solving foreign ones. A society built on the vow and the local ties that such vows engender would be so engrossed in the development of the goods of the locality that imperialism would be seen as an unwanted distraction. Local pride would then take the form of patriotism rather than a belligerent nationalism.

Chesterton viewed the imperialism of the later Victorian era as having a numbing effect on the sentiments of the common people. The people began the nineteenth century believing that their leaders were motivated by the desire to protect all that was good in England and not by personal gain or expansion of power. At the end of the nineteenth century, England had ceased to be a nation preoccupied with the love of their local interests and had been swept into a shallow nationalist outlook.

Chesterton alludes to this change in the following expert from his autobiography:

> Nobody can measure the change who was not brought up, as I was, in the ordinary newspaper-reading middle-class of the Victorian Age. We need not argue here about all that may be said for and against the idealism, or the optimism, or the sentimentalism, or the hypocrisy or the virtue of the Victorian Age. It is enough to say that it rested solidly on some social convictions, that were not only conventions. One of them was the

belief that English politics were not only free from political corruption, but almost entirely free from personal motives about money.... I know that my Victorian uncles did not know how England is really governed. But I have a strong suspicion that if (they) had known, they would have been horrified and not amused; and they would have put a stop to it somehow. Nobody is trying to put a stop to it now.[24]

To put it simply, Chesterton saw that the common people had been led astray by their leaders and ended by accepting the world these latter had created for them. When Chesterton speaks of Cobbett's protest against the loss of England's local rural customs, he is citing an early prophetic voice which was sympathetic to the commoners and which was above all patriotic. Cobbett was patriotic in the sense of loving what made England attractive to the ordinary people who lived there: Its green meadows, the tradition of individual liberty, the fellowship rooted in Christianity, and the uniquely nuanced quality of its language and literature.

Chesterton thought the Industrial Revolution brought a plutocracy whose imperialistic ambitions managed to cancel out most of these reasons for appreciating England. Migration to the cities made the appreciation of natural beauty a rarity. The increasing power of money and politics made the individual vote less effective. The established church became the province of self-interest rather than charity. But literature remained an area where the common man could still find a voice reflecting an England worth loving.

Chesterton points to the English preference for literary expression over other forms when he compares the English revolution to the revolution in France:

The upshot was that though England was full of the revolutionary ideas, nevertheless there was no revolution. And the effect of this in turn was that from the middle of the eighteenth century to the middle of the nineteenth the spirit of the revolt in England took a wholly literary form. In France it was what people did that was wild and elemental; in England it was what people wrote.[25]

In *The Victorian Age in Literature*, Chesterton outlines the attitudes of the literary writers toward their time. They react based on their own personalities and the formative influences in their background. Matthew Arnold, the son of a schoolmaster, looks to culture and educational reform while for Charles Dickens the common man reacts as a kind of mob in revolt against injustice. Newman, steeped in the classics and the church fathers, reacts with a lucid, magisterial prose. These writers are some examples Chesterton used to outline the spirit of the age. He does not believe in the idea that the artist is a solitary worker unconcerned with the moral climate of the place in which he lives.

Because literature is a product of the mind and an expression of spiritual realities, it is particularly suited to tracing the spiritual landscape. Chesterton was aware that the spiritual order was not tied to the chronological order, but followed its own independent laws instead. The task he set for himself in his study of Victorian literature was to present a necessarily incomplete picture of something essentially impossible to capture in its entirety.

His attitude toward this task tells us a great deal about his attitude toward history in general. Chesterton knows that his attempt will fall short of the goal but he nonetheless attempts it anyway. His strong antipathy toward the rationalist school of history is rooted in this real incommensurability between the spiritual realities, i.e., human ideas and motivations, and the limitations of language.

> Now in trying to describe how the Victorian writers stood to each other, we must recur to the very real difficulty noted at the beginning; the difficulty of keeping the moral order parallel with the chronological order. For the mind moves by instincts, associations, premonitions, and not by fixed dates or completed processes. Action and reaction will occur simultaneously: or the cause will actually be found after the effect. Errors will be resisted before they have been properly promulgated: notions will be first defined long after they are dead. It is no good getting the almanac to look up moonshine; and most literature in this sense is moonshine. Thus Wordsworth shrank back into Toryism, as it were, from a Shellyan extreme of pantheism as yet disembodied. Thus Newman took down the iron sword of dogma to parry a blow, not yet delivered, that was coming from the club of Darwin. For this reason no one can understand tradition, or even history, who has not some tenderness for anachronism.[26]

When Chesterton speaks of the mind moving "by instincts, associations, premonitions, and not by fixed dates or completed processes", he is focusing on the immediacy of attraction and repulsion rather than the discursive processes of the intellect. For example, when Chesterton speaks of Charles Dickens tasting the spirit of his age and spitting it out, he was alluding to the moral quality that is essential to understanding the character of any period in history. The idea of loving and hating what one ought to love and hate is first put forth in Aristotle's *Ethics* as the concept of moral virtue. It is this understanding of what makes for human character that informs the novels of someone like Jane Austen, and provides the raw material for most of literature. Chesterton ranges over this moral landscape in his study of Victorian literature in an attempt to give insight into its foundations. Just as Aristotle was accustomed to beginning his study of a particular moral virtue by asking what the common man thought, so does Chesterton pay consistent attention to the reactions and actions of the English people when trying to understand the moral climate in which they lived.

The delineation of character is the province of literature, but it is also the essential ingredient of any fully realized history. The recitation of chronological sequence is only the very minimum of historical information needed to grasp the truth of a given era and is quite capable of obscuring some of the truth as well. Speaking of the doctrine of historical progress espoused by Macaulay, Chesterton rebuts what he calls the "fallacy of the forerunner":

> Nevertheless the fallacy of the 'forerunner' has been largely used in literature. Thus men will call a universal satirist like Langland 'a morning star of the Reformation', or some such rubbish; whereas the Reformation was not larger, but much smaller than Langland. It was simply the victory of one class of his foes, the greedy merchants, over another class of his foes, the lazy abbots. In real history this constantly occurs; that some small movement happens to favor one of the million things suggested by some great man; whereupon the great man is turned into the running slave of the small movement.[27]

The common thread that ties together the ideas of character and anachronism is the primacy of the spiritual over the material. Character concerns the movements of the spirit of individual persons or groups of people, and anachronism is a rebuke to a too rigid insistence on a purely linear conception of history. Chesterton is always aware that history is the fruit of human thought and action at work in a specific place with specific characteristics. However, the ramifications of these fruits of human character extend outward like the ripples of water that emanate from a disturbance, intersecting with an immense number of other emanations. The metaphor is not linear but rather all-encompassing.

One example of Chesterton's reliance on this spiritual reading of history is his comparison of Victorian England and nineteenth-century America. In his travels to the United States, he observed the flexibility of American society along with its openness to human creativity:

> There is one real advantage that America has over England, largely due to its livelier and more impressionable ideal. America does not think that stupidity is practical. It does not think that ideas are merely destructive things. It does not think that a genius is only a person to be told to go away and blow his brains out; rather it would open all its machinery to the genius and beg him to blow his brains in.[28]

The American society was more youthful in spirit and therefore prone to risk-taking and a non-conventional use of ideas. On the other hand, England seemed to Chesterton to be suffering from a spiritual senility:

> The Victorian Age suffered from being, not the time in which the domestic spirit was at its highest, but the time when it was at its lowest. It was an age of doubt rather than of doctrine; and that was precisely the reason why, in most cases, the convictions only remained as conventions. [29]

In one sense, history for Chesterton is the record of the differences among people. But for these differences to be made clear, it is necessary first to observe the climate and the terrain, the religious beliefs and other ideals, the festivals and the family life of the population. Through an observation of these qualities, one can penetrate the creeds and traditions that form their roots. As he says in *The Victorian Age in Literature,* "The moment we differentiate the minds, we must differentiate by doctrines and moral sentiments."[30]

If Chesterton saw the Middle Ages as a time of dogma and the Victorian age as a time of convention, he was not unaware of the many reactions to these conventions. He could not help but notice that one writer, Charles Dickens, stood out in his championing of the common man's stubborn adherence to what he cherished:

> And it is right to say that when more sophisticated Victorians set up fads like fences, and established new forms of narrowness, that flood of popular feeling, that was a single man, burst through them and swept on. He was a Radical, but he would not be a Manchester Radical, to please Mr. Gradgrind. He was a humanitarian, but he would not be a platform Pacifist, to please Mr. Honeythunder. He was vaguely averse to ritual religion; but he would not abolish Christmas, to please Mr. Scrooge. He was ignorant of religious history, and yet his religion was historic. For he was the People, that is heard so rarely in England; and, if it had been heard more often, would not have suffered its feasts to be destroyed. [31]

Chesterton sees Dickens as someone who intuitively responded to the life that he saw around him. Dickens' theatrical background was the appropriate complement to this very developed power of intuition. He was like Chesterton in his ability to see the truth of a situation without the need for many steps of discursive reasoning. He also had the expressive talent to give life to these perceptions. In *A Handful of Authors*, Chesterton remarks that Dickens' characters resonate so deeply with the common people of England that they join the ranks of the very few literary creations that assume a permanent life.

> Nevertheless the fact remains that Mr. Conan Doyle's hero is probably the only literary creation since the creations of Dickens which has really passed into the life and language of the people, and become a being like

John Bull or Father Christmas. . . . In no other current creation except Sherlock Holmes does the character succeed, so to speak, in breaking out of the book as a chicken breaks out of the egg. The characters of Dickens had this capacity.[32]

Dickens was the portrait painter of the multiplicity of characters that peopled England. He was suited by talent and temperament to hold the mirror up to his age and show it as it truly appeared. The fact that his age readily embraced his characters and took them to heart is indicative of his ability to imitate reality accurately and convey it with an artfulness that delighted his audiences. In his *Poetics*, Aristotle speaks of the universal human pleasure taken in a good imitation, whether it be something inherently distasteful like the macabre shop of Mr. Venus or something naturally pleasant, such as the character of Agnes Wickfield. Dickens had a broad range of portraiture coupled with an incisive understanding of human motivation.

The imitative power of Dickens is most obviously put in the service of justice. Novels like *Bleak House* and *Hard Times* provide a view of things as they should not be and thus stimulate a reaction that might encourage reform. The effect of Dickens' writings comes under the heading of patriotism in the sense that it evinces a love for what England could be if its virtues were strengthened and its vices were eradicated. This quality of Dickens coincides with Chesterton's definition of the true patriot. He was someone whose love for his country endured even when his country was not lovable.

Chesterton had many occasions in his own life to experience the truth of Dickens' characterizations. In his *Autobiography*, he recounts the following example:

> But indeed these first memories and rumours suggest that there were a good many Dickens characters in the days of Dickens. I am far from denying the inference; that a good many Dickens characters are humbugs. It would not be fair to say all I have said in praise of the old Victorian middle-class, without admitting that it did sometimes produce pretty hollow and pompous imposture. A solemn friend of my grandfather used to go for walks on Sunday carrying a prayer book, without the least intention of going to church. And he calmly defended it by saying, with uplifted hand, "I do it, Chessie, as an example to others." The man who did that was obviously a Dickens character. And I am disposed to think that, in being a Dickens character, he was in may ways rather preferable to many modern characters. . . . Hypocrisy itself was more sincere. Anyhow, it was more courageous.[33]

This was an example of the following of outward forms long after the inner meaning had been abandoned. As we have seen already, Chesterton noticed that the unconsciously held traditions of a society may extend their influence for many years during which the conscious principles are opposed to these traditions; or there may be a mixing of logically incompatible customs the inconsistency of which remains invisible to their practitioners. This kind of situation points out the asymmetrical and nonlinear understanding of history that Chesterton espoused. Incidentally, Chesterton would find the asymmetrical human behavior of the man carrying the prayer book to be a prime example of what makes history interesting and unpredictable, and not insignificantly, inaccessible to the methods of empirical science.

Chesterton seems to think that a familiarity with the bewildering variety of human character and temperament is an indispensable factor in obtaining an imaginative grasp of the past because one has to be on the inside of people in order to see them as they truly are. The people who are perfect never let anyone inside them and, as a result, remain impenetrable to any real understanding. Chesterton touches on the difference between the perfect but unreal person versus the imperfect but authentic individual in speaking about *David Copperfield*:

> Let the clever people pretend to govern you, let the unimpeachable people pretend to advise you, but let the fools alone influence you; let the laughable people whose faults you see and understand be the only people who are really inside your life, who really come near you or accompany you on your lonely march toward the last impossibility. That is the whole meaning of Dickens; that we should keep the absurd people for our friends. And here at the end of David Copperfield he seems in some dim way to deny it. He seems to want to get rid of the preposterous people simply because they will always continue to be preposterous.... I repeat, then, that this wrong ending of David Copperfield is one of the very few examples in Dickens of a real symptom of fatigue.[34]

Chesterton would prefer that Micawber not be sent away and that Mr. Dick be given a more important position. Perhaps even Mr. Creakles should be kept around. Chesterton finds these preposterous people to be the essential fabric of every society and every country. To send them away would not result in the betterment of society but in its abolition. We can get a glimpse here of his sense of the absurdity of eugenics. The fact is that every human being is a little absurd, and while travel may be broadening in one sense, it is often in staying at home in one's locality that real growth can be achieved. Chesterton thinks that people are worth getting to know well because it is only after time and experience with people's idiosyncrasies that one can see the good hidden behind the shortcomings.

This insistence on not only being satisfied with one's locality and neighbors, but also coming to delight in them, is a theme that Chesterton approaches from many angles. In his literary criticism of Dickens,

Chesterton appoints him as the voice of the people. This is because Dickens gave voice to so many different kinds of human beings while almost never failing to rejoice in the existence of each one. Even Dickens' evil characters, such as Quilp or Bill Sykes, are presented as really taking hold of their existence as something that they cherish. They may be types of Aristotle's vicious man who actually delights in doing wrong, but they are never desultory or despondent. In creating these kinds of characters, Dickens showed himself to be an artist who understood that existence in all its infinite variety was something first of all to be cherished for its own sake.

In his *Autobiography*, Chesterton touches on this theme that is so fundamental to his thinking when he breaks down the distinction between the optimist and pessimist, and points to something that unites them on a deeper level.

> . . . no man knows how much he is an optimist, even when he calls himself a pessimist, because he has not really measured the depths of his debt to whatever created him and enabled him to call himself anything. At the back of our brains, so to speak, there was a forgotten blaze or burst of astonishment at our own existence. The object of the artistic and spiritual life was to dig for this submerged sunrise of wonder; so that a man sitting in a chair might suddenly understand that he was actually alive, and be happy. [35]

If this were the object of the artistic and spiritual life, then Charles Dickens had been successful many times over in his novels through their rich description of humanity, concretely realized in so many highly localized creations. Paradoxically, by creating such localized, vivid characters, Dickens was able to confer upon them a kind of immortality that most other writers were unable to achieve. Mr. Pickwick, Wilkins Micawber, and Miss Havisham are examples of characters who live outside of time, so to speak, and remain static. For this reason, Chesterton credits Dickens with making more than literature—in essence making a mythology.

Mythology captures the heroic qualities that are admired by the common people. Chesterton thinks that each person has within himself the capacity to be great. What he admires most about Charles Dickens is that he had the same intuition and used his literary talent to create a gallery of characters who stand out as heroic. Their heroism resides in the fact that they have souls which, when developed, bring to light their own individuality.

Chesterton points out this faith in the greatness of every man as one of Dickens' most important qualities in the following passage from *Charles Dickens, The Last of the Great Men*:

> We shall consider Dickens in many other capacities, but let us put this one first. He was the voice in England of this humane intoxication

and expansion, this encouraging of anybody to be anything. His best books are a carnival of liberty, and there is more of the real spirit of the French Revolution in 'Nicholas Nickleby' than in 'A Tale of Two Cities.' His work has the great glory of the Revolution, the bidding of every man to be himself; it has also the revolutionary deficiency; it seems to think that this mere emancipation is enough. No man encouraged his characters so much as Dickens. 'I am an affectionate father,' he says, 'to every child of my fancy.'[36]

By encouraging "anybody to be anything", Dickens shows that he is the very opposite of the materialist. He believes that each man has a creative principle inside him that, if encouraged, can allow him to become someone great. It follows from this that Dickens would not be in agreement with any determinist theories of history. When his characters are evil, it is because they have made bad choices. Similarly, when they are very good, it is because they have chosen well. Neither Emerson's Oversoul nor Buckle's scientific rationalism would find a sympathetic hearing from Charles Dickens.

Anyone, however ordinary, can make a contribution to his or her locality and country. But this contribution will only come about if each person is encouraged to become what his nature and talent indicate. This is why Dickens fills his books with such a vibrant array of characters, and dotes on all on them. If the story is a garden, then he is the good gardener who looks after all of the plants and cultivates them to grow to their full stature.

Chesterton sees this very Dickensian spirit at work in the early years of the Victorian era:

> The spirit of the early century produced great men, because it believed that men were great. It made strong men by encouraging weak men. Its education, its public habits, its rhetoric, were all addressed towards encouraging the greatness in everybody. And by encouraging the greatness in everybody, it naturally encouraged superlative greatness in some. Superiority came out of the high rapture of equality.[37]

This idea that human greatness arises out of human equality places Dickens firmly on the side of democracy. In his novels, democracy shows itself to be disorderly and unpicturesque. However, it is in this messy workshop that heroes are produced. The reason for this is that the liberty and equality that flourish in democracy foster human development, while an impermeable aristocracy or totalitarian system stifles it. In his philosophy of history, Chesterton sees democracy as the political system most favorable to the development of individuals in both localities and society as a whole.

A democracy encourages each person to cultivate his talents along with the specific raw material offered by his locality. In the broadest sense, this raw material includes not only the obvious natural qualities of the place, but the cultural endowments as well: for instance, the language, the literature, and the spiritual patrimony. Only democracy gives the necessary hope that such cultivation will be allowed to bear fruit. When this process is permitted to take root, it produces love for what is distinctive to a certain place.

Chesterton saw the fruits of this kind of liberty to be the ordinary things associated with any particular country, such as their clothing, food, songs, and stories. These are the kinds of detail that Dickens was so adept at describing and bringing to life in his novels. He could present the dark side of English education in Professor Gradgrind or Mr. Creakles and yet remain optimistic that improvement was possible.

This is an example of how Dickens fits Chesterton's understanding of patriotism. The patriot for him is someone who is discontented with the faults of his country but continues to love it nonetheless. This is opposed to the nationalist who is blind to his country's faults, and takes an aggressively competitive stance toward other countries. Dickens rarely looks beyond England in any of his books because he sees so much to admire in his own country as well as so much that is in need of curing. He happily spends his time and talent cultivating the flowers of his own garden, pruning and fertilizing the unproductive and wilting plants. He never thinks of stealing plants from his neighbor's garden.

Instead, such a man with good motivations will observe the different flowers in his neighbor's garden and admire them without wanting to acquire them. Chesterton describes this type of scenario as follows:

> It is a great mistake to suppose that love unites and unifies men. Love diversifies them, because love is directed towards individuality. The thing that really unites men and makes them like to each other is hatred. Thus, for instance, the more we love Germany the more pleased we shall be that Germany should be different from ourselves, should keep her own ritual and conviviality and we ours. But the more we hate Germany the more we shall copy German guns and German fortifications in order to be armed against Germany. The more modern nations detest each other the more meekly they follow each other; for all competition is in its nature only a furious plagiarism. As competition means always similarity, it is equally true that similarity always means inequality. If everything is trying to be green, some things will be greener than others; but there is an immortal and indestructible equality between green and red.[38]

The point Chesterton makes about love is essential to an understanding of his philosophy of history. The simple principle that love is directed toward individuality underlies his great emphasis on locality. Chesterton saw specificity as the indispensable requirement for any sort of attraction. This has to do with the idea of form as boundedness and enclosure. It is only by marking off a certain definite area and cultivating within that area a love for a particular place or persons that patriotism grows.

In his emphasis on the love for local things, Chesterton reveals an underlying philosophical vision that is founded on the idea of form. If form is understood to be that which makes a thing what it is, and no other thing, then a philosophy of history that accepts this truth will necessarily stress the importance of individual men and specific localities. Dickens is an author who stresses both of these things to a very high degree.

Like the junk collector in *Our Mutual Friend,* Dickens could not bear to part with anything. He had great sensitivity in expressing the many differences among his characters, as well as considerable descriptive power in conveying the multiplicity of detail in atmosphere and setting. He could not bring himself to simplify his novels because they were imitating the complexity and diversity of reality. Dickens' common sense told him that a novelist who wanted to write about Victorian England would have to write many novels, with numerous complicated plots and subplots, and many colorful characters. He could not collapse an almost infinitely complex world into simple reductionism.

Chesterton praises Dickens for this refusal to oversimplify reality. In *Appreciations and Criticisms of the Works of Charles Dickens*, Chesterton states the following:

> The time will soon come when the mere common-sense of Dickens, like the mere common-sense of Macaulay (though his was poisoned by learning and Whig politics), will appear to give a plainer and therefore truer picture of the mass of history than the mystical perversity of a man of genius writing only out of his own temperament, like Carlyle or Taine.[39]

The difference between Dickens and Carlyle is that the latter was so consumed with his own ideas that he imposed them on any reality that attracted his gaze. He tended to see everything through the lens of Carlyle. Dickens, on the other hand, was like a chameleon who took on the characteristics of whatever aspect of reality attracted his attention. As a result, he was able to present a complex and paradoxical reality of England, without exhausting it—but without diluting it either.

Chesterton had this same power of appreciating and expressing the complexity of historical reality. The critic John Coates acknowledges Chesterton's openness to the intricacies of writing about the past. These complexities arose not only from the nature of the reality to be described, but also from the character of the historian himself. As Chesterton makes clear in his comments about Carlyle and Macaulay, the temperamental attributes of the historian will always influence the history that he writes.

> In fact Chesterton's sense of the past is a complex and evolving appreciation of its many lights and shades, acknowledging half-tones, embracing

the moral and psychological difficulties of writing history in general, understanding and assessing his own emotional predilections, in particular. It is an intellectual exploration, sustained by an increasing self-knowledge, thoughtful and, in a sense, morally impressive.[40]

In Chesterton's view, the greater historical understanding comes from the widest possible openness to reality on the part of the historian. This was an attribute of Dickens's temperament, at least regarding his own England. He reacted to his time the way that any ordinary Englishman would have reacted, but he was blessed with extraordinary gifts of artistic expression. Chesterton did not see Dickens as someone who arrived on the scene of the Victorian age with a set of preconceived theories, but rather as someone who had a desire for all things genuinely English and a repugnance for whatever was not. As he said in his essay on Dickens entitled *"The Great Gusto"*, "Dickens is outside the Victorian enclosure, not so much because he was original as because he was traditional."[41]

Dickens was traditional in the sense that he took what was handed over from the past and tried to understand why it had been considered worth preserving by his ancestors. He was not the sort of person who first tears down a fence and later asks why the fence was built. He gave the dead just as much credit for being intelligent as he gave to those who were his contemporaries. As Chesterton was famously wont to say, there is no reason why democracy should be limited to the living. Just because a man is dead is no reason to disregard his contribution.

In this sense Dickens was similar to Chaucer. They were both quite open to the varied human types of their own time, and ready to accept them on their own terms. This acceptance implied that both Chaucer and Dickens were eager to place themselves imaginatively into the minds and motivations of different human characters. Both men were well acquainted with facts, Chaucer through his many diplomatic dealings with the court and Dickens through his own colorful upbringing. As Chesterton describes in *Charles Dickens, The Last of the Great Men*:

> It must be remembered . . . that there was something about the county in which he (Dickens) lived, and the great roads along which he traveled that sympathized with and stimulated his pleasure in this old picaresque literature. The groups that came along the road, that passed through his town and out of it, were of the motley laughable type that tumbled into ditches or beat down the doors of taverns . . .[42]

Both Chaucer and Dickens were also able to move beyond facts to the spirit that lay behind them and write narratives that captured the spirit of their respective times. If Chaucer saw the nascent ramifications of commerce at its very beginnings, Dickens was allowed to chronicle the effects when commerce was full-grown. Chaucer saw the widespread influence of

Christian faith when it permeated English life, and Dickens was there to record its moribund stages.

Both writers were truthful about the faults of people, but neither became misanthropes because of it. Their ability to so vividly record the human panorama was directly related to their affection for the multiplicity of human characters. In both Chaucer and Dickens, Chesterton sees the great power of the literary approach to understanding and recording history. This power resides in capturing the features of a particular locality, whether it is fourteenth-century Sussex or nineteenth-century London.

In their carefully delineated portraits of individual characters, Chaucer and Dickens captured what was highly specific and at the same time what was universal. It was specific because it partook of the manners and customs of their age, but it also had a universality because of the underlying human nature that unites all ages. This ability to move back and forth between the extremely specific and the enduring universal is one aspect of the quality of balance that is shared by Dickens, Chaucer, and Chesterton. They do not leave out any characters as trivial or unimportant. At root, they are all democrats in the sense that they will give every man his say. And they will go even further and try to understand and sympathize with why he says it.

It is an easy step from this quality of balance to Chesterton's own partiality for paradox. Like Chaucer and Dickens, he sees that reality is wonderfully complex and he is unwilling to sacrifice the complexity for the sake of a simplifying order that eliminates mystery. As Chesterton says in *The Uses of Diversity*, a true understanding of the past must make room for everything:

> It is sillier not to see that a man can fire off a gun for a prejudice as well as he can for an ideal. I disagree with the Orangemen; I don't disagree with the Nationalists; but I deny neither. I sympathize with the Labour revolt; I don't sympathize with the Feminist revolt; but I deny neither. Then, again, both these latter tendencies have succeeded in colliding violently with another reality, the priests of the ancient popular creed of Ireland. They achieved that catastrophe, not because they did not believe the creed, but because they could not even believe that it was believed.[43]

In this passage, Chesterton speaks of the need to accept every historical movement and personage as worthy of being taken seriously. Because Chaucer and Dickens took the whole world seriously, they were able to avoid the extremes of either ideology, which sees only a partial view, or pseudo-scientific impartiality that is less than human. For Chesterton, history is about tracing the endless varieties of human nature as they manifest themselves in specific localities, and this outline can best be achieved through the instrument of literature.

4   The Creative Lens

Chesterton's novels and poetry convey a distinctive view of history. In particular, *The Ball and the Cross*, *The Man Who Was Thursday*, and *The Napoleon of Notting Hill* are novels with themes of consequence to Chesterton's philosophy of history. As more than one critic has pointed out, Chesterton uses the novel form as an opportunity to lay out the details of competing philosophical understandings of the world. It is not uncommon for his characters to represent a particular philosophical position in a way that is akin to the allegorical characters of a Bunyan or a Spenser. An example of this would be the pacifist in *The Ball and the Cross* who intervenes between MacIan and Turnbull in their attempts to settle their differences by swordplay. The pacifist mouths the philosophy of Tolstoy and provides the novel's two main characters with an opportunity to attack his philosophical position. Literary devices such as this have caused some critics to fault Chesterton's novel writing for its attempts to depict different philosophical opinions rather than to tell a good story. In essence, he is criticized for subordinating the aesthetic requirements of a work of art to the demands of outlining and defending his particular viewpoints.

This criticism has some merit: it is true that *The Ball and the Cross* and *The Napoleon of Notting Hill* do not rise to the level of aesthetic perfection evidenced by novels such as *Brideshead Revisited* or *Portrait of a Lady*. Nevertheless, this clear difference in artistic quality fails to answer the interesting question of why Chesterton chose to use a story form to convey his philosophical ideas in addition to bare expository prose. In the case of each novel, the reader is presented with conflicting views of the world whose opposition provides the driving force for the plot. The conflict is not so much resolved as it is shown in a fuller context by means of the narrative form of the novel. Perhaps Chesterton favored the form of a story because it was the only way to present the living reality of the worldviews that he was trying to unravel. If he had been satisfied with an abstract exposition of the positions of pacifism, atheism, and militarism, to take three examples, he would not have been able to convey as vividly the hold that these views have on particular persons in local places at given times.

Such an abstracted treatment would so remove the humanity from the ideas that the imaginative force of Chesterton's positions and, consequently, their persuasive power, would be largely lost. On the whole, Chesterton's treatment of ideas in his novels is a good example of what Flannery O'Connor meant when she said that a story is a way of saying something that can't be said in any other way.

There is a general impulse that moves the physical scientist to strip the material world to the bare bones of its numerical qualities of length and breadth to more efficiently manipulate it through mathematics. This same impulse compels Chesterton to clothe his philosophical notions in the garb of specific people and places so that they might be more fully understood. What might appear to be subjective to the empirical scientist is exactly the thing that Chesterton wishes to focus on most closely. It is precisely the subjective that makes up the material of the novel in the sense that characters are most fully realized to the degree that they assume highly delineated form.

Chesterton understood that ideas do not exist apart from the men and women that think them and are influenced by them. He saw the movement of history as an interplay of human personality and ideas together with all the distinctive qualities of local language and customs. And while generalizations may be possible in the physical sciences because of the nonspiritual quality of matter, they are less useful in the understanding of history due to the spiritual nature of man. Chesterton touches on this point in the preface to *The Napoleon of Notting Hill* when he speaks of the futility of human prophecy:

> The human race, to which so many of my readers belong, has been playing at children's games from the beginning, and will probably do it till the end, which is a nuisance for the few people who grow up. And one of the games to which it is most attached is called, "Keep tomorrow dark," and which is also named (by the rustics in Shropshire, I have no doubt) "Cheat the Prophet". The players listen very carefully and respectfully to all that the clever men have to say about what is to happen in the next generation. The players then wait until all the clever men are dead, and bury them nicely. Then they go and do something else. That is all. For a race of simple taste, however, it is great fun.[1]

Men and women will never be predictable in the rigid sense of the physical sciences because they have free will. This spiritual quality of freedom is the reason why history cannot be a science in the same sense as physics.

In *The Everlasting Man*, Chesterton elaborates on the inadequacy of a purely scientific approach vis-à-vis the subjective understanding of human history, and shows the corresponding necessity for an instrument that is adequate to the human material that history offers for study:

> So long as we neglect this subjective side of history, which may more simply be called the inside of history, there will always be a certain limitation on that science which can better be transcended by art. So long as the historian cannot do that, fiction will be truer than fact. There will be more reality in a novel; yes, even in a historical novel. [2]

If the form of the novel is the literary model most suited for the subjective and the individual, then it is also the most fitting vehicle for the expression of historical ideas.

In his novel, *The Ball and the Cross*, Chesterton's two main characters are Evan MacIan and (Mr.) Turnbull. MacIan is a representative of Roman Catholicism and Turnbull is an atheist. Both men are unlike most of their fellow men in that they take their viewpoints seriously, and are willing to risk their lives because of them. The story unfolds between these two poles of belief and unbelief. During the course of their attempt to duel with each other, both antagonists come to the realization that they have something important in common that none of their fellow men share. As they flee from the authorities who try to stop them from fighting, they encounter others who represent different ways of looking at the world. While the others primarily hold views as theories, Turnbull and MacIan follow the practical consequences of their beliefs more thoroughly.

One of the faults of MacIan is that he does not have much of a sense of humor. As he and Turnbull are attempting to evade the police so they can carry on with their duel, Turnbull wonders aloud whether MacIan can keep up the pace. When MacIan replies that he can run quite well, Turnbull responds, "Is that a qualification in a family of warriors?" MacIan answers, "Undoubtedly. Rapid movement is essential."[3] Turnbull laughs at his adversary's inability to see the joke in his question.

The lack of humor that characterizes MacIan is a quality that prevents him from seeing the different aspects of the same reality. Since understanding a joke involves seeing two meanings at once, MacIan's narrowness makes for a single-minded opponent, but one who eventually will be enriched by his enemy's personality. Turnbull the atheist is not completely bad, but is rather a human being with reasons for his position.

Chesterton takes the qualities of each character and allows them to highlight the defects and strong points of the other. It is characteristic of his approach to show that MacIan the believer has something to learn from Turnbull the atheist. Similarly, in Chesterton's personal relationships with his friends, he was able to argue the merits of their positions while remaining amicable, and even admiring the force of their convictions. A good example of this is Chesterton's friendship with the socialist George Bernard Shaw. Chesterton's characters reflect this same quality.

Chesterton sees the truth that both Turnbull and MacIan look at reality in different ways, and though one might expect him to side more with MacIan, in one sense at least he does not. When the two duelists find that their flight from the police has brought them to the French-speaking Isle of St. Loup, they both praise the French for different reasons. Turnbull extols France because it is the country of skepticism and rebellion:

> 'France, that has always been in rebellion for liberty and reason. France, that has always assailed superstition with the club of Rabelais or the rapier of Voltaire. France, at whose first counsel table sits the sublime figure of Julian the Apostate. France, where a man said only the other day those splendid unanswerable words, 'we have extinguished in Heaven those lights which men shall never light again.'
>
> 'No,' said MacIan, in a voice that shook with a controlled passion. 'But France, which was taught by Saint Bernard and led to war by Joan of Arc. France that made the crusades. France that saved the Church and scattered the heresies by the mouths of Bossuet and Massillon.'[4]

All that each character has to say about France is of course true, depending on the point of view of the observer. Chesterton is not inclined to relativism, though he seems to be saying that the reality of a people is not so easily encompassed, but rather contains more than one paradoxical element.

Turnbull expresses this paradoxical notion when he says, "France, where reason and religion clash in one continual tournament."[5] He sees reason as the perpetual challenger and adversary of religion, whereas MacIan is so lacking in the sense of irony that he has difficulty seeing that the same passionate nature that makes the French capable of religious fervor also produces their fiery skeptics. Both he and Turnbull are paying their respects to the French national temperament as it resonates most strongly with their own individual temperaments. However, their running conversation provides the reader with a type of verbal tennis match in which points are scored on both sides. It is part of Chesterton's plotting device that the antagonists are never allowed to bring their sword fight to a fatal conclusion: For if that were to happen, they would cease to be effective embodiments of the paradoxical structure of people and nations.

An example of this manner in which both characters shed light on the same reality can be seen in Turnbull's comment as he realizes that they are fighting near a wayside crucifix of the kind only found in predominately Catholic countries.

> Turnbull glanced at the crucifix with a sort of scowling good humor and then said: 'He may look and see His cross defeated.'
>
> 'The cross cannot be defeated,' said MacIan, 'for it is Defeat.'[6]

MacIan may not be able to see the irony in Turnbull's jokes, but he has a clear-sightedness about the truths of his own religion. The great reversal that is found at the heart of Christianity involves a paradox in which the immortal God became mortal and changed the ultimate symbol of failure into something signifying victory. This point in the novel is similar to many others in that it is a progression from two distinct perspectives toward a settled, if not coalescing, complementarity.

Before too long, both Turnbull and MacIan are confronted with a group of English policemen who try to convince them that they are still under English jurisdiction, albeit on a French-speaking island in the channel. When they realize their mistake, the two elude the policemen and resume their flight from the authorities who are bent on stopping them. The role of the policemen is at odds with the outlook of both Turnbull and MacIan for one important reason: The policemen are the instruments of a society that lives only in the present and is unmindful of the past.

When Turnbull and MacIan are brought before the magistrate at the novel's beginning, they are accused of disturbing the peace. MacIan has broken the window of Turnbull's printing shop because of a blasphemous placard insulting the Virgin Mary that has been placed inside the window. Both men are sincere enough in their beliefs to want to fight each other in defense of them, but the magistrate considers their quarrel a kind of comedy. The magistrate states his views in the following passage:

> 'For Heaven's sake, man,' he said, 'don't talk so much. Let other people have a chance (laughter). I trust all that you said about asking Mr. Turnbull to fight, may be regarded as rubbish. In case of accidents, however, I must bind you over to keep the peace.'[7]

The magistrate is unconcerned with the deeper questions of Turnbull's atheism and MacIan's Christian faith. He is only concerned with the here and now of avoiding conflict and preserving external order. Perhaps he is even unaware of his own title and the veneration of tradition that is implied in it. He has nothing to teach the two combatants other than an admonition to get along with each other. The educative function of the law is completely lost on the magistrate, and he is not so much magister as he is a minister or servant of the status quo.

Directly before he encounters Turnbull's offending sign, MacIan comes upon the statue of Queen Anne in front of St. Paul's Cathedral. Thinking it to be a figure of the Virgin Mary, he pauses in respectful deference, and is somewhat surprised at the lack of veneration of the people passing by.

> He did not understand that their one essential historical principle, the one law truly graven on their hearts, was the great and comforting statement that Queen Anne is dead.[8]

MacIan is strongly tied to the living traditions of his past and reacts to his surroundings as a part of that tradition, and not as a deracinated individual. For him, the dead are alive in spirit and do not cease to have influence merely because they are no longer walking among the present generation.

The peace and order of the present moment were naturally not as important to a man such as MacIan as loyalty to true traditions of the past, if only because those traditions were handed down for a good reason. They were the most valuable possessions of his ancestors. His great-grandfather had died at Culloden and his own father had refused to attend to Queen Victoria when she visited Scotland. Chesterton comments:

> Evan himself had been of one piece with his progenitors and was not dead with them, but alive in the twentieth century. He was not in the least the pathetic Jacobite of whom we read, left behind by a final advance of all things. He was, in his own fancy, a conspirator, fierce and up to date. In the long, dark afternoons of the Highland winter he plotted and fumed in the dark. He drew plans of the capture of London on the desolate sand of Arisaig.[9]

One of the implications of MacIan's adherence to a living tradition is the presence of a supernatural world. The ideas and actions of those who came before him are not dead relics to be discarded, but rather the living fabric of history whose protagonists still live on in another world which continues to take a vital interest in the most recent incarnation of humanity.

MacIan is the child of a specific locality in the Scottish Highlands, with the temperament and interests that such a place cultivates. Like his forefathers, he is a patriot with a love for the northern land of his birth and at the same time, a patriot of the vastly more expansive land peopled by his countless ancestors in the timeless world above nature. In one sense, MacIan lives in a far larger world than either the magistrate or Turnbull. The magistrate is indifferent to the more expansive world above nature that is inhabited by his ancestors, whereas Turnbull is not indifferent but rather actively opposed to it. Turnbull has his flag planted in a definite world, but since it is considerably smaller that MacIan's, he derives the strength of his opposition from a desperate defense of the only world that he knows.

Chesterton aligns the fierce nationalist disposition with those who do not have a belief in the larger world of the supernatural. It is difficult to be a patriot and let others live as their local customs dictate when one's world is circumscribed by one's own birth and death. What Chesterton once called the democracy of the dead, or the belief that one's fathers should not be ignored merely because they were no longer living, is exactly the kind of outlook that frees MacIan to be a lover of his own locality and traditions, without being a hater of everyone else's. His world is large and rich enough to satisfy him, and he knows that he does not have to desperately gain control of all of this relatively short-lived experience of nationhood.

Turnbull is a revolutionary in his desire to overturn what he considers the oppressive weight of religious belief and the injustices that it brings. Near the end of the novel when he is imprisoned in the asylum along with MacIan, Turnbull comes under the direct control of the master, a character representative of the devil. The master provides Turnbull with a vision of the world being cleansed by a revolutionary fire that destroys not only authorities such as popes and kings, but also those who were poor and imperfect. When Turnbull asks the master why even these latter are being destroyed, he replies that they are simply a dead weight on progress. The master explains:

> 'You see, these people were much too tired and weak even to join the social war. They were a definite hindrance to it.'
> 'And so you are simply burning them out?'
> 'It does seem absurdly simple," said the man, with a beaming smile, 'When one thinks of all the worry and talk about helping a hopeless slave population, when the future obviously was only crying to be rid of them. There are happy babes unborn ready to burst the doors when these drivellers are swept away.'[10]

Turnbull ends by rejecting this infernal cleansing of the weak and unfit because he has more of MacIan's respect for life, as well as a keen sense of injustice and a desire to put things right. MacIan for his part has his own encounter with the master, and is shown a vision of a world in which Christianity is protected by the sword and where perfect order is maintained by the strong authorities of church and state. It is a vision calculated to appeal to his love of traditional order and benevolent authority.

When MacIan witnesses an old man struck across the back by one of the authorities for moving too slowly, he questions the master and receives the following response:

> 'The people must be taught to obey; they must learn their own ignorance. And I am not sure,' he continued, turning his back on Evan and looking out of the prow of the ship into the darkness, 'I am not sure that I agree with your little maxim about justice. Discipline for the whole society is surely more important than justice to an individual.'[11]

At this point, MacIan is inclined to admire a society that respects the traditional order of church and state, but he cannot accept the price of personal injustice that this entails in the master's plan. Both MacIan's and Turnbull's visions show what happens when worthy goals are isolated and pursued with a kind of single-mindedness that precludes the balancing and sustaining of goods that have been excluded. Left to himself, MacIan might easily become a zealous patriot and extreme isolationist without regard for differing viewpoints—in short, he would favor a theocracy. On the other hand, Turnbull is inclined toward a strong nationalism whereby the state overturns all inequities and enforces a radical equality based on a rejection of traditional religion. But the vision shows Turnbull that the state would do no better than MacIan's theocracy in providing justice and respect for the human person.

It is through their adventure in mutual antagonism that Turnbull and MacIan come closer to the reality that they are both neither completely right nor completely wrong in their approach to human society. They are each telling a partial truth and they come to see the deficiencies in their views through their contact with each other. What the two men have in common is their desire to fight for their beliefs and their conviction that within these lie the keys to a better world. This is precisely why the master—the figure of the devil—is threatened and wishes to imprison them.

There is one other figure in the book, however, Father Michael, whom the master fears more than anyone else. He is detached from the things of the world, and looks on the struggles for better society with a certain amount of equanimity born of this disinterestedness. He is put in the most secure area of the asylum because his detachment holds the greatest possibility for real change and improvement in human society. As Chesterton points out in *A Short History of England,* the monks and nuns of western history have acted as benevolent unmarried aunts and uncles to the world:

> It is not merely flippant to say that monks and nuns stood to mankind as a sort of sanctified league of aunts and uncles. It is a commonplace that they did everything that nobody else would do; that the abbeys kept the world's diary, faced the plagues of all flesh, taught the first technical arts, preserved the pagan literature and above all, by a perpetual patchwork of charity, kept the poor from the most distant sight of their modern despair. [12]

Michael has embraced the cross in both its horizontal and vertical aspects, and is therefore more capable of seeing and accepting the paradoxical elements of the truth which Turnbull and MacIan only partially see. As MacIan says to Turnbull near the end of the novel when he is trying to explain his new insights:

> 'You must give me time,' said MacIan, quite patiently, 'for I am trying to tell the whole truth. I am trying to tell more of it than I know.'[13]

In the end, MacIan and Turnbull both appeal to Father Michael to save them from their partial view of human history. In the character of Michael, Chesterton sums up in *The Ball and the Cross* an important aspect of his philosophy of history, namely that apparently contradictory elements such as patriotism and nationalism can be reconciled when one is disinterested enough to see the truths and excesses of both:

> 'I had a dream,' said Turnbull, thickly and obscurely, 'in which I saw the cross struck crooked and the ball secure——'

'I had a dream,' said MacIan, 'in which I saw the cross erect and the ball invisible. They were both dreams from hell. There must be some round earth to plant the cross upon.'[14]

In another of his novels, *The Napoleon of Notting Hill*, Chesterton uses two characters, Auberon Quin and Adam Wayne, to further explore the nuances of patriotism and nationalism. Set in the year 1984, the novel unfolds as Quin is made king through the random selection process used by the England of the future. Everything at this age became mechanical because the people had expected to get as good a government from random selection as they would from an ordered process. The English had lost faith in revolutions and preferred to lead their lives under the authority of an official functionary while their lives remained unchanged. Chesterton paints a picture of a country which is content to merely retain the status quo and not hope for anything more. The people are simply going through the motions of living, with a kind of animal vitality and no belief in a transcendent order.

Into this staid environment appears Adam Wayne, a patriotic citizen of the suburb of Notting Hill, who steadfastly refuses to accede to the wishes of the larger metropolis where his neighborhood is concerned. Since none of his fellow countrymen have cared much about change, it comes as a shock to them that such a man would defend his neighborhood with his life.

The situation arises from an unexpected decision by Quin the king, who is fond of jokes more than anything else, and decides to enliven the dull lives of all the English citizens by reviving the medieval customs for each town and locality. Each would be required to have a banner, a coat of arms, and a city wall with a gate and guards. He is inspired to do this by a chance meeting with a little boy with a wooden sword. The boy confronts the king, and declares that he is the king of the castle—a declaration that the king takes as the beginning of something serious. The king describes his decision:

> 'A revival of the arrogance of the old medieval cities applied to our glorious suburbs. Clapham with a city guard, Wimbledon with a city wall. Surbiton tolling a bell to raise its citizens. West Hampstead going into battle with its own banner. It shall be done. I, the king, have said it.'[15]

The king does this because he does not want the memory of the people's origins to die out. He also does it for the sense of fun it would provide. Above all, the king wants to bring about a keener sense of local patriotism in the various principalities of London.[16]

The reaction of the people is mixed. Some are incredulous and others are indignant. Nevertheless, he orders the medieval revival to be carried out and everyone has to comply. The leaders, or provosts, of each suburb are to be chosen using the same principle of random selection. Quin's friends, the politician James Barker and the clerk James Wilson, are made provosts of South Kensington and Bayswater respectively. They are more concerned with leading in a steady, pragmatic way, and consider the heraldic trappings to be a nuisance.

When these provosts attempt to create a road project that will traverse several suburbs, they are opposed by Adam Wayne, the provost of Notting Hill. He refuses to make way for the new road by the destruction of Pump Street in his district, which he holds particularly dear because of his early childhood memories of playing on the street. When Wayne comes before King Quin to oppose the road, the king is delighted that someone has taken his attempts to revive local patriotism to heart. Just as Wayne proudly wears the bold, red colors of his heraldic emblem, Quin feels he has proudly restored the beauty of an earlier period in history.

Chesterton is making the point that Quin and Wayne are artists as compared to the other provosts who are dead to the beauty of the world. As such, Quin and Wayne recognize the startling quality of the reality around them. In particular, Chesterton contrasts Wayne's assumption of his medieval role and his noble sense of a higher meaning with the rationalist, self-serving dispositions of Barker and Wilson. Chesterton does not so much see the medieval period of history as empty of any self-seeking or of a narrow vision, but he understands it to be a time when people could be inspired to fight for transcendent truths and not just for self-interest.

When he presents the case for Pump Street before the king, Wayne points out the difference between his own motivation and that of the other provosts:

> 'O, you kings, you kings,' cried out Adam, in a burst of scorn. 'How humane you are, how tender, how considerate. You will make war for a frontier, or the imports of a foreign harbor; you will shed blood for the precise duty of lace, or the salute to an admiral. But for the things that make life itself worthy or miserable—how humane you are. I say here, and I know well what I speak of, there were never any necessary wars but the religious wars. There were never any just wars but the religious wars. There were never any humane wars but the religious wars. For these men were fighting for something that claimed, at least, to be the happiness of a man, the virtue of a man. A crusader thought, at least, that Islam hurt the soul of every man, king or tinker, that it could really capture. . . . If, as your rich friends say, there are no gods, and the skies are dark above us, what should a man fight for but the place where he had the Eden of childhood and the short heaven of first love?' [17]

Wayne's philosophy echoes Chesterton's comments in *The Everlasting Man* on what motivates a soldier (see Chapter 1). It is neither the imports of a foreign harbor nor a warm water port that will motivate a person to action, but rather those things that have touched him most personally; his ties to God, people, and the place of his birth.

In contrast, the other provosts—especially Barker and Wilson—speak of promoting the public interest, and seem to be concerned at least superficially with the judicious arrangement of citizen affairs. However, they do not have any particular loyalty to a place or a God. The common thread that connects these latter is that they are gratuitous: No one chooses his creator just as no one chooses where he is born. What differentiates Adam Wayne from the other provosts is that he has wholeheartedly embraced the gratuitous in his life and finds it worthy of being defended. Barker and Wilson, on the other hand, go about their business looking at the world as something to be molded to their will. For them, it is merely raw material for the exercise of their own desires. This is why they are portrayed as the enemies of the imagination, especially for artists such as Quin and Wayne.

Chestertown juxtaposes the different approaches of these characters in other scenarios as well. Before he is proclaimed king, Auberon Quin together with his fellow clerks, James Barker and Wilfred Lambert, has a chance meeting in a London street with the deposed president of Nicaragua. Over lunch they learn that the Central American nation has become one of the world's last small republics to be subsumed into a larger state. In the course of conversation, Barker proclaims " . . . my sympathies are with no nation."[18] He is also the adamant proponent of England's present systematization of life. He favors the random mechanical processes by which the king is chosen, and prefers predictable governance by dull, bureaucratic functionaries. The salient feature of Barker's ideal state is the absence of choice. In his view, the exercise of human freedom has to be systematically minimized, leaving little room for spirits such as Auberon Quin or the Nicaraguan president (who dies a few days later, worn out by his struggles on behalf of his country).

In the midst of the rigid systems so admired by Barker, Quin finds an unusual way to assert his freedom. He pursues jokes with the same fervor that Barker promotes the impersonal government by system. This continual humor first provokes his colleagues to frustration, and then to anger when they realize he will never consent to be serious. But behind his absurd humor, Quin has found a way to defend the human freedom that is under attack in the England of 1984. When, much to the outrage of Barker and Lambert, Quin is named king through the random selection process, Barker pleads with him to be serious and receives the reply, "You ask me why I don't care for anything else. Can you tell me, in the name of all the gods you don't believe in, why I should care for anything else?"[19] Barker can only resort to general admonishments concerning the importance of the public interests while Quin sweeps them away with the answer that he is always joking because it is his choice to do so.

Like Melville's Bartelby, Quin asserts his human freedom in the face of those who have considered it to be of no importance. Since Barker and his fellow clerks have reduced the notion of God to a superstition, and abolished the nation in favor of a system of mechanistic regularity, both the philosophical foundation for human freedom and the area for its exercise have been greatly reduced. Quin's reaction is similar to that of the Nicaraguan president when the latter responds to Barker's championing of a controlling system of efficient government: "My only objection is a quite personal one. It is, that if I were asked whether I would belong to it, I should ask first of all, if I was not permitted, as an alternative, to be a toad in ditch. That is all. You cannot argue with the choice of a soul."[20]

In the characters of Quin and Wayne, Chesterton is working out some of the human implications for a world without transcendence. When Barker responds to the Nicaraguan president's reply he says, "Of the soul . . . I cannot pretend to say anything, but speaking in the interests of the public—-" At this Quin excuses himself and goes outside convulsed in laughter to repeat over and over, "speaking in the interests of the public . . ." It is clear that his reaction highlights the absurdity of Barker's claim to know what is best for his fellow countrymen. The rationale behind Barker's government is that there is no principle of spiritual autonomy, and no soul. Such a rationale leaves little room for freedom, and any claim to know what is good for others is eventually revealed as a thinly disguised arbitrariness. In reality, it is the will of some men, such as Barker, that determines the possibilities of action for other men.

One of the story's great ironies is that the system in which Barker puts his faith allows a king such a Quin to take power. Quin's incessant humor unmasks Barker's delusion that the common good can be achieved without the cooperation of human freedom. Quin chooses to be silly, and there is nothing Barker can do about it but attempt to carry on in businesslike manner while hoping that the king's jokes will not cause too much interference. The situation is exacerbated for him when Quin recognizes a kindred spirit in Wayne, leaving Barker to deal with yet another human spirit who defies his philosophy.

By contrasting the figures of Barker, Quin, and Wayne, Chesterton highlights his view of the origins of a nation. Without a multiplicity of human choice, the nation can easily become a hollow form that is instrumentalized by the wishes of a few. Each human person who participates in the building up and cherishing of his locality contributes to the vitality and strength of the nation. However, this participation and cooperation implies a love that is synonymous with choice. Wayne wants Pump Street to remain Pump Street because he loves it. Quin wants to help him because he recognizes, dimly at first and then more clearly, that Wayne is enacting the vision of life that he, the king, has been instinctively promoting with his stubborn humor.

In the dedicatory poem Chesterton places at the novel's beginning, he envisions the sky as a blue cap that perfectly fits every locality. It is cherished by each locality as its own, yet it is universally shared by everyone.

The paradox illustrated here is that nations can flourish, and by implication, human persons as well, only when each local place is loved for its own sake. Each member of the neighborhood of Notting Hill can find something to protect and cultivate while allowing the others to do the same. In a world informed by Barker's philosophy, such a scenario is made impossible because human freedom is the prerequisite for love, and without love there is no reason to align one's interests with another's.

Both Quin and Wayne share in common their appreciation of the colors and contours of reality. For them, it is enough that reality is endlessly rich to make it worth reveling in. At the beginning of the book, when Quin is following his two friends Barker and Lambert down the street, he imagines their tailcoats to be the heads of dragons and becomes completely taken with this image. His vivid imagination enables him to see things beyond the strictly functional. This is another way of saying that he is open to an understanding of the gratuitous quality of reality. Quin takes delight in the colors and textures of the heraldic banners and liveries because they are not purely utilitarian. They point to the beauty and nobility of the ideals they symbolize: a gratitude for the surroundings into which one is born, and a desire to defend and improve them.

The king differs from Wayne in that he has a keener sense of the incongruity between the serious materialism of men like Barker and Wilson and the transcendent symbolism of their colorful medieval garb and ceremony. This is why he laughs at them when they become irritated by his love of such things. Adam Wayne, on the other hand, is somberly absorbed in the importance of his position as provost because he loves Notting Hill and more particularly, Pump Street, with a fierce loyalty that comes from having grown up there. For him, the streets and buildings of Notting Hill have become as permanent and enduring as nature. He could not imagine the world without them.

> Adam Wayne as a boy had for his dull streets in Notting Hill the ultimate and ancient sentiment that went out to Athens or Jerusalem. He knew the secrets of the passion, those secrets which make real old national songs sound so strange to our civilization. He knew that real patriotism tends to sing about sorrows and forlorn hopes much more than about victory. He knew that in proper names themselves is half the poetry of all national poems. Above all, he knew the supreme psychological fact about patriotism, as certain in connection with it as that a fine shame comes to all lovers, the fact that the patriot never under any circumstances boasts of the largeness of his country, but always, and of necessity, boasts of the smallness of it.[21]

Here again Chesterton ties patriotism with locality suggesting that the two are inseparable. In his development of the character of Adam Wayne, however, he explores the connection between this love of a specific locality and the sensitivity to beauty. For Wayne, Notting Hill is the most significant gift that he has been given; he is grateful for it and, as a result, will fight to protect it.

One could argue that patriots are grateful children and nationalists are spoiled brats. Nationalists want all the toys of the other children in addition to their own, and they are never quite satisfied. Barker and Wilson are uneasy with their positions as provosts of South Kensington and Bayswater, and are eager to put their road project through the locality of Notting Hill. They see nothing noteworthy or special about their own towns because the material aspect is what is most important to them. Just as Adam Wayne has become habituated to seeing the beauty and gratuity of his surroundings from a young age, so Barker and Wilson have become accustomed to instrumentalizing their surroundings rather than seeing them as ends in themselves. The primary fact for Wayne when he looks at the details of Notting Hill is that it is wonderful in its specificity. For example, when he looked at the pointed railings of the iron fences along Pump Street in his youth, he dreamt of spears:

> As a child, Wayne had half unconsciously compared them with the spears in pictures of Lancelot and St. George, and had grown up under the shadow of the graphic association. Now, whenever he looked at them, they were simply the serried weapons that made a hedge of steel round the sacred homes of Notting Hill. He could not have cleansed his mind of that meaning even if he tried. It was not a fanciful comparison, or anything like it. It would not have been true to say that the familiar railings reminded him of spears; it would have been far truer to say that the familiar spears occasionally reminded him of railings.[22]

The conflict over the road cannot be settled without fighting because Adam Wayne has no intention of giving up his beloved Pump Street, and Barker and Wilson are confident that their superior numbers will defeat any troops that Wayne can muster. The king assumes more the role of an observer, though he seems to favor Adam Wayne. Although outnumbered, Wayne's army of Notting Hill enters into battle and triumphs through ingenuity and their intricate knowledge of the neighborhood. They extinguish the gaslights at a crucial moment and, as a result, their enemies attack each other in the darkness.

A second and decisive victory is achieved when Wayne threatens to open the floodgates of the Notting Hill water tower and inundate the armies sent against him. The other neighborhoods capitulate and Notting Hill is finally preserved. The interesting twist is that once the other neighborhoods have seen Notting Hill's resolve, they in turn want to preserve the integrity of their own localities. They even go so far as to suggest that Notting Hill has become arrogant in its successes, and might try to start an empire. In rallying together to prevent Notting Hill from becoming too powerful and eclipsing their own neighborhoods, they begin to be proud of their hometowns much in the same way as Wayne did. Barker and Wilson start to wear their uniforms with distinction, and take new delight in their weapons and traditions. Chesterton shows through this latter development that when people fight for something, they begin to love the cause.

The book closes with a rather surreal scene involving a discussion between Wayne and King Quin. They remark how Wayne is perpetually serious and the king is always seeing the humor and irony in life. Eventually, they agree that they represent the two sides of the human mind, or a way of looking at things that is incomplete until complemented:

> When dark and dreary days come, you and I are necessary, the pure fanatic, the pure satirist. We have between us remedied a great wrong. We have lifted the modern cities into that poetry which everyone who knows mankind knows to be immeasurably more common than the commonplace. But in healthy people there is no war between us. We are but the two lobes of the brain of a ploughman.[23]

These themes of locality, patriotism and nationalism are explored in another of Chesterton's works, *The Ballad of the White Horse*. In it, Chesterton tells the story of King Alfred's fight against the marauding Danes who sought to overrun England in the ninth century. The ballad is not purely traditional in that it is not passed on by oral custom but rather it is written down by a single author. For this reason, it would properly be called a literary ballad, but nevertheless partakes of some of the qualities of a traditional ballad. The origin of the word ballad can be found in the Provençal word, *balada*, which means a dancing song.[24]

The songlike quality of Chesterton's work is apparent in its strong alliterative quality and the extensive use of thematic repetition. In its length and content, the ballad shares some of the qualities of an epic poem. There is the presence of the supernatural, the great hero, and national or racial themes, along with a lengthy and serious narrative. These qualities indicate that Chesterton's ballad is really a hybrid of two poetic forms. Perhaps he chose to combine the obvious epic nature of the poem's contents with the ballad form out of a desire to lay some stress on the elements of song and play that are essential to his theme.

Although the poem begins with a recounting of the serious events whereby Alfred the king has been driven to the tiny island of Athelney, the Danes have not yet prevailed over all of England. Alfred's island becomes his small kingdom. While praying there one day, he has a vision of his childhood. His mother is showing him a very small book in which a blue-robed Virgin Mary is pictured with the infant Christ at play:

> And he saw in a little picture,
> Tiny and far away,

> His mother sitting in Egbert's hall,
> And a book she showed him, very small,
> Where a sapphire Mary sat in stall
> With a golden Christ at play.[25]

Alfred asks the Virgin whether the Danes will stay forever or if they will be driven away. She responds that all Christians must live by faith and cannot know what the outcome of their efforts will be. Far from making Alfred despair, this answer encourages him to go out and gather the chiefs of Wessex to resist the Danes. His response illustrates what is perhaps the central paradox of the poem; from very small and seemingly hopeless beginnings come great things. When the English are most beaten down is when they are on the verge of winning. Also, the element of unconcern that characterizes play is the same element that has to characterize the efforts of the English against the Danes. They have no sure promise of victory, but must fight on without caring too much about the outcome. The king's vision of the small Christ child is at once an emblem of unconcerned play coupled with omnipotence. The Virgin addresses him as follows:

> I tell you naught for your comfort,
> Yea, naught for your desire,
> Save that the sky grows darker yet
> And the sea rises higher.
>
> Night shall be thrice night over you,
> And heaven an iron cope.
> Do you have joy without a cause,
> Yea, faith without a hope?[26]

When King Alfred goes to find the three chiefs, Mark, Colan, and Eldred, he offers them a chance to fight against the Danes once more. The chiefs represent the three prominent racial and historical influences of Britain; Mark the Roman influence, Colan the Celtic influence, and Eldred that of the Saxons. They ask him why they should fight against the superior force of the Danes, to which he can only repeat the answer of the Virgin that the sky grows darker yet and the sea rises higher.

Alfred finds two of the chiefs, Eldred and Mark, reluctant to leave the peaceful arts of agriculture and masonry that are their occupations when they are not fighting. Chesterton underscores the ties and security that they are leaving behind. Eldred's farm is rude and poorly cultivated, but a place of warmth and welcome:

> The smoke of evening food and ease
> Rose like a blue tree in the trees
> When he came to Eldred's farm.[27]

The Creative Lens 99

Eldred is skeptical because he has suffered so many losses at the hands of the Danes before:

> Why should my harmless hinds be slain
> Because the chiefs cry once again,
> As in all fights, that we shall gain,
> And in all fights we fail . . .
>
> Your scalds still thunder and prophesy
> That crown that never comes;
> Friend, I will watch the certain things,
> Swine, and slow moons like silver rings,
> And the ripening of the plums.[28]

Chesterton is illustrating that despite their reluctance to leave the reassuring certainty of the cycles of nature and the comfort of their hearths, at some level they understand the inevitable need to oppose the Danes lest they be swallowed up.

Initially, Mark is not inclined to leave the land he has cultivated and made fruitful. His grape arbors and olive trees are more dear to him than the thought of embarking on a military campaign whose outcome is far from certain.

> Long look to the Roman on the land;
> The trees as golden crowns
> Blazed, drenched with dawn and dew empearled,
> While faintlier colored, freshlier curled,
> The clouds from underneath the world
> Stood up over the downs.
>
> 'These vines be ropes that drag me hard,'
> He said. 'I go not far . . .
> Guthrum sits strong on either bank
> And you must press his lines
> Inwards, and eastward drive him down;
> I doubt if you shall take the crown
> Till you have taken London town.
> For me, I have the vines.' [29]

Although Mark does not decide right away to join Alfred, he later shows up at battle.

Colan's reaction to Alfred's request is different from that of both Eldred and Mark. While their responses are bound up with their love of the localities that they have cultivated, Colan lives in a cave in the wilderness and is scornful of Alfred's request. This is probably because the Celts were driven into the western part of England by the invading Saxons. While Colan shares Alfred's faith in Christianity, he states that, unlike the Saxons, the Celts are strong enough to fail and survive. Responding to the words of the vision, he says in the warlike manner of his people, the Celts:

> And if the sea and sky be foes,
> We will tame the sea and sky.[30]

Thus, Colan decides to join Alfred. The common thread that ties together the decisions of Eldred, Mark, and Colan to join the king in opposing the Danes is a Christian belief that responds to Alfred's vision. This common thread is important enough to bind together former enemies and men of varying temperaments. Chesterton uses this as an example of how Christianity, even on the local level, can serve as a kind of supranational glue.

After gathering the chiefs to his cause, Alfred makes his way to the camp of the Danes. He has disguised himself as a wandering minstrel. Alfred is taken to Guthrum, the Danish leader, after being heard playing his harp. The Danish chiefs take Alfred's harp and sing their own songs that celebrate their bloodthirsty exploits in battle and their nihilism. The songs of these chieftains lack hope because the gods that they worship do not offer them any goods beyond transitory power over their enemies and the rough enjoyment of the spoils of war. Guthrum is sad on his throne because he has the sensitivity of temperament to understand the limitations of such a worldview. When the chieftains return the harp to the disguised Alfred, he sings his own song in response to theirs. The song contains the following words:

> What have the strong gods given?
> Where have the glad gods led?
> When Guthrum sits on a hero's throne
> And asks if he is dead?[31]

Alfred's song is an answer to the paradox of Guthrum's despair. The Dane is the conqueror of his enemies, but inside he feels as though he is not alive. The Wessex men that follow Alfred are outnumbered in the battle, but they feel internally fortified because of their vision of life. The goodness of their own local world resonates so deeply within them that they do not see their own misfortune as a definitive failure. The Wessex rebels fighting the Danish hegemony are influenced by the common Christian belief in the goodness of creation. The enduring and personal power that stands behind creation is reason enough for them to be cheerful in the face of what looks to be certain defeat.

Paradoxically, their love of the very small, whether it be Alfred's island of Athelney or the olive groves and farms of Mark and Eldred, is a stronger motivation than the rapacious and far-ranging depredation of the

Danes. The defenders of Wessex are patriots and the Danes are nationalists. Alfred provides a concise connection between the goodness of creation and the apparent hopelessness of his position in the last verse of his song to the Danes:

> For our God hath blessed creation,
> Calling it good. I know
> What spirit with whom you blindly band
> Hath blessed destruction with his hand;
> Yet by God's death the stars shall stand
> And the small apples grow.[32]

The Danes laugh at his song because they have no place in their outlook for a god who is weak enough to die, much less bring life to his creation through such a defeat. The fact that Alfred delivers his message to the Danes with a song is significant because the music moves the whole person while words speak to the intellect and less directly, to the heart. Chesterton is quite aware of the importance of song in both his choice of the poem's form and in his references to music in the ballad.

After singing for the Danes, Alfred makes his way to the meeting place where he will join up with the Wessex chiefs. There he comes upon the hut of a poor woman and sits down to rest by the fire. He is weary and hungry, and the woman takes him to be a beggar and gives him the task of watching the fire in exchange for a cake to eat. As Alfred sits by the fire, he pities the woman and thinks how her lowly estate reminds him of God's own impoverishment when he became man. While pitying the woman her lowly position, he falls asleep leaving the food to fall into the fire. He is awakened by the angry woman's slap across his face. For a minute, he stands up and looks at her with thoughts of torture, as he is, after all, the king. But after his initial reaction, Alfred laughs out loud and startles all the gathered soldiers who have come to meet him.

> 'Now here is a good warrant,'
> Cried Alfred, 'by my sword;
> For he that is struck for an ill servant
> Should be a kind lord.

> 'He that has been a servant
> Knows more than priest and kings,
> But he that has been an ill servant,
> He knows all earthly things.'[33]

Alfred then explains that he will wear the red mark of the woman's blow as an emblem against the pride of the Danes because he is the "first king known of heaven that has been struck like a slave."³⁴ In Chesterton's philosophy of history, a king such as Alfred is the true embodiment of the patriotic ruler. This is because he is not motivated by pride and self-serving motives, but rather by a desire to defend and cultivate a greater good than himself. This representation also conforms to Millon-Delsol's understanding of authority (discussed in chapter one), which envisions power orientated toward the common good rather than used in the service of selfish interest. Such a vision would find a distinguished representative in the person of King Alfred.

Having marshaled his men, Alfred then leads them to face the Danish invaders who have assembled at Ethandune. The Danes look on the tattered, ill-clothed and ill-fed men that Alfred has gathered, and are moved to laughter. When the Danish warrior Harold draws his bow to send an arrow at the Wessex men, Colan the Gale hurls his sword at Harold and kills him. This gesture of throwing away the sword inspires Alfred to declaim on the fundamental difference between his men and the Danes.

> For this is the manner of Christian men,
> Whether of steel or priestly pen,
> That they cast their hearts out of their ken
> To get their hearts' desire.³⁵

For Alfred, it is enough that they are giving everything they have to the battle despite the uncertainty of the outcome. He and his men are following the lead of the vision that inspired him at the poem's beginning. The paradox of their situation is that they are rendering themselves vulnerable but not giving up the fight, irrespective of the great odds against them.

Out of all his fellow warriors, Alfred is the most simple and childlike in his approach to the battle. Chesterton sums this up by saying that "Alfred fought as gravely as a good child at play."³⁶ This is because he refuses to give up, approaching the battle with both the detachment and the seriousness of one who is playing a game. This scenario is reminiscent of the King Quin's description to Wayne in *The Napoleon of Notting Hill* of their respective playfulness and seriousness as the two sides of the whole man's outlook. Just as the child whose building blocks fall down continually picks them up and begins again—undeterred by the temporary setbacks—so does Alfred pick himself up and renew his efforts against the Danes after each defeat. The combined quality of detached seriousness that makes this effort possible is not found among the Danes because they worship victory and power above everything else, and so are prone to despair. They have looked at the weakness inside themselves and turned away from it to exalt in their power over others. By contrast, Alfred looked inside himself and became humble and therefore was protected from despair. The Danes are the perennial nationalists in locating their strength outside themselves before they have found it within.

The climax of the poem comes when Alfred, deprived by the deaths in battle of his lieutenants Eldred, Colan, and Mark, renews a hopeless charge against the vastly superior Danes. Surrounded by his enemies who mock his fragile position, Alfred dodges the spear thrust of the Danish champion, Ogier, and the spear lodges in a tree. Before he can retrieve his lance, Ogier is cut down by Alfred. As the tide of the battle turns, Alfred sees the vision of the Blessed Virgin above them. The Danes are eventually defeated, and Guthrum, seeing the outcome of the battle, becomes convinced of the truth of Christianity and receives Baptism:

> For not till the floor of the skies is split,
> And hell-fire shines through the sea,
> Or the stars look up through the rent earth's knees,
> Cometh such rending of certainties,
> As when one wise man truly sees
> What is more wise than he.[37]

Book Eight of the *Ballad* is entitled, "The Scouring of the Horse". The gigantic white horse that is emblazoned on the earth overlooking the scene of the Danes' defeat is in need of continual scouring if it is not to become overgrown with weeds. This cleaning of the white horse is symbolic of the need for continuous renewal if the hard-won freedom of the English is to be preserved. The love of their locality motivated the Wessex men to defend their land against the Danes, and eventually to overcome them. Had the three chiefs given in to their initial reticence and not followed Alfred's lead, they would have permanently lost the land that they loved to the Danes. Even more importantly, they would have allowed their posterity to be oppressed under the Danes' nihilistic way of life.

In emphasizing the scouring of the horse, Chesterton brings his understanding of locality from the synchronic to the diachronic. It is well for Colan, Eldred and Mark to love their distinctive local beauty, but it is quite another thing to preserve it for their descendants. Here is where Chesterton's philosophy of history ties patriotism to locality. To love one's locality is to be a patriot in the partial sense, but it is only when this love moves one to defend it that the fullness of patriotism is achieved. In this way, the true patriot is made part of something larger even than his own life. He assumes a place in the history of his nation, however small it may be, because he has transcended the limitations of his locality for the sake of a greater good; namely, that the beauties that he loves may not be lost to his descendents.

If history is the story of a people, then it cannot end with the close of a single chapter but must go on until the entire story is told, encompassing as it does the lives and times of many persons. Chesterton's other well-known ballad entitled *Lepanto* is similar to *The Ballad of the White Horse* in its ultimate concern with the diachronic element. The poem tells the story of the Christian nations of Europe banding together to face their common enemy, the Muslim Turks. The last naval battle under oars took place in the Gulf of Lepanto near Greece on October 7, 1571. Like *The Ballad of the White Horse*, the poem features a heroic figure in Don John of Austria who provides leadership to a disparate group of warriors against a common enemy. Here, however, the enemy is not the nihilistic, pagan Danes but the adherents of Islam. The action of *Lepanto* is of a narrower scope than *The Ballad of the White Horse*. It paints vibrant pictures of the contrast between the Muslim and Christian worlds. Chesterton's artistic eye for color and detail is given full play in describing the historical associations that give concrete vividness to the antagonists in the battle.

Pope Pius V responds to the Muslim threat to Cyprus by calling on the Christian princes of Europe to defend their lands against further Muslim incursions, since at this point all of the North African coast is under their control. The Sultan of Byzantium's arrogant laughter is contrasted with the distress of the pope who, seeing Christendom in the fragments of the Reformation, looks for a champion. Just as *The Ballad of the White Horse* conveys the hopelessness of King Alfred's plight when faced with the fierce Danes, so does the overwhelming might of the Muslims contrast with the disunity of the Christian nations of Europe.

The guiding spirit of the Muslim forces is Mohammed, who looks down from his paradise and directs his followers against the same threat that came out of Europe during the crusades. Chesterton's description of the opulence of the Muslim paradise is an example of his ability to use imagery to portray dramatic differences in historical worldviews. Chesterton puts the following words in the mouth of Mohammed:

> And he saith, 'Break up the mountains where the hermit-folk can hide,
> And sift the red and silver sands lest bone of saint abide,
> And chase the Giaours flying night and day, not giving rest,
> For that which was our trouble comes again out of the west.
> We have set the seal of Solomon on all things under sun,
> Of knowledge and of sorrow and endurance of things done;
> But a noise is in the mountains, in the mountains, and I know
> The voice that shook our palaces—four hundred years ago:
> It is he that saith not 'Kismet'; it is he that knows not Fate;
> It is Richard, it is Raymond, it is Godfrey in the gate!
> It is he whose loss is laughter when he counts the wager worth:
> Put down your feet upon him, that our peace be on the earth.'[38]

One of the important themes being presented by Chesterton in the passage above is the Christian understanding of providence versus the Muslim's exaltation of God's will over all human attempts to act freely. Mohammed is the advocate of an historical determinism because he emphasizes the power of his God to such an extent that the efficacy of individual human wills is made insignificant by comparison. In urging his followers to be relentless in their destruction of the Christians, Mohammed evinces the puritanical zeal that characterizes a simple religion. Chesterton is probably not unaware of the irony whereby the Christians are preparing a Europe fragmented by the voluntarism of the Calvinists and Lutherans to do battle against an enemy whose own brand of voluntarism opposes them.

The Protestant emphasis on the absolute sovereignty of God left almost no room for any real interest in a genuine human history. With roots struck deep in the nominalism of the late Middle Ages, the Protestant sects of the Reformation found it difficult to see human wills as decisive seats of secondary causality. Catholic Europe does not suffer from this problem precisely because the balance is maintained between God's omnipotence and man's freedom. Chesterton's poem grasps the fundamental significance of this basic difference between the Muslim and Christian views of the world. The rising action of the poem's dramatic structure is centered on the pope's attempts to unify the individual wills of the European princes.

As is turns out, the key to this unification is found in the unlikely person of Don John of Austria. He is not an obvious leader because of his youth (24 years old in 1571) and because of his precarious claims to his throne. Despite this, his personal boldness and persuasive powers render him able to unite the fractious Christian princes, most notably the Italians and the Spaniards.

> Dim drums throbbing, in the hills half heard,
> Where only on a nameless throne a crownless prince has stirred,
> Where, risen from a doubtful seat and half attainted stall,
> The last knight of Europe takes weapons from the wall.[39]

The emphasis on the small and partial beginnings of the resistance to the Turkish threat is in keeping with Chesterton's belief that the most historically effective movements tend to be the result of the interplay between personal choice and Providence. The forces that Don John pieces together are less a juggernaut than a collection of rivals who have to be persuaded of the persistent threat posed by their common enemy.

The element of persuasion is worth examining more closely because it highlights several ideas that are essential to Chesterton's philosophy of history. The first idea concerns the importance of human freedom. Because Chesterton sees history as a tapestry woven from an immense number of human wills, his poem about a pivotal event in human history must emphasize this. A chief way that he does this is through juxtaposition and contrast. Elizabeth I of England is preoccupied with her own vanity while Charles IX of France is unmoved by religious concerns, and the Sultan of Byzantium, popularly known as Selim the Sot, is arrogantly confident of the fanatical numbers of his navy.

106 *The Historical Imagination of G.K. Chesterton*

>And the Pope has cast his arms abroad for agony and loss,
>And called the kings of Christendom for swords about the Cross.
>The cold queen of England is looking in the glass,
>The shadow of the Valois is yawning at the Mass;
>From evening isles fantastical rings faint the Spanish gun,
>And the Lord upon the Golden Horn is laughing in the sun. [40]

Such a picture of a variety of personalities and dispositions illustrates the interplay between different players and the decisiveness of their individual freedoms. It is up to Don John of Austria to appeal to these various free human agents and, if he can, persuade them to act. The poem unfolds with alternating references to the various human agents, whether the monarchs of Europe or the Sultan in Byzantium, and the persistent and decisive movement of Don John toward the confrontation in the Gulf of Lepanto.

Don John's movements are like the basso continuo of a Baroque concerto while multiple themes play around him. Having made up his mind to fight, Don John provides one dependable theme of the poem, a theme which Chesterton presents through repetitive parenthetical phrases: "*(Don John of Austria is going to the war.) . . . (Don John of Austria is girt and going forth.) . . . (Don John of Austria is armed upon the deck.) . . . (Don John of Austria is hidden in the smoke.) . . . (Don John of Austria has burst the battle line.) . . . (Don John of Austria rides homeward with a wreath.)* "[41]

This device provides a picture of the simultaneity of human freedoms. Set against the dependable theme of Don John's decisive action are the secondary themes of European princes influenced by rivalries, Protestant theology, personal shortcomings, and a multiplicity of local concerns. Don John's personal influence is an attempt to make effective the theme of a European unity based on a common Christian heritage. The picture of this historical event shows the complexity and yet intelligibility of history; complex because of the interaction of many themes, but intelligible because of the common human nature that gives rise to the decisions forming events.

Another device that Chesterton employs is the poem's insistent alliteration and rhythmic drive that help to convey the determination of Don John in the face of the overwhelming numeric superiority of the Turkish fleet. The form of the poem is not insignificant because it is meant to be recited aloud and is written with a strong rhetorical quality.

>Sudden and still——hurrah!
>Bolt from Iberia!
>Don John of Austria
>Is gone by Alcalar.[42]

Chesterton could have written a summary of the historical events surrounding the Battle of Lepanto in an essay form. However, he chose to use a poetic form with an intensely aural appeal. In light of the aforementioned rhetorical qualities, it seems clear that the poem is meant to be performed orally to achieve the greatest effect. Unlike poems such as *Paradise Lost* or *In Memoriam*, Chesterton's work harkens back to an oral tradition in which a poem was meant to be recited aloud in order to be fully understood.

Both temperamentally and artistically, Chesterton was predisposed to the oral expression of his ideas. His preferred forms for his historical poems bear witness to this preference. The *Ballad of the White Horse* is written in the form of a song and *Lepanto* follows a similar form. Several important things follow from the songlike quality of the poem. One quality of a poem with a strong oral form is the ability to convey the past as something alive. There is a well-known anecdote about a buffalo told by the famous scholar of orality, Walter J. Ong. He would tell his students that you could smell, see, touch and taste a buffalo, and the buffalo could be dead. But if you hear a buffalo, he would say, watch out—because the buffalo is certainly alive. The mark of active power is sound.

The oral devices used in Chesterton's poem not only include alliteration and repetition but also, of course, rhyme. Rhyme was of paramount importance to Chesterton because it has a way of emphasizing the truth of what is being said: It serves as a kind of oral notarization. In an essay entitled, *The Romance of Rhyme*, Chesterton makes the following point:

> In another aspect, rhyme is akin to rhetoric, but of a very positive and emphatic sort; the coincidence of sound giving the effect of saying, 'It is certainly so.' Shakespeare realized this when he rounded off a fierce or romantic scene with a rhymed couplet.[43]

Psychologically, Chesterton uses rhyme to drive home the actuality of the events he is recounting in a much more effective way than the essay form.

Historically, rhyme was a primary device whereby poets could bring to mind the lengthy verses of epic poetry for their pre-literate listeners. Such a device emphasizes the importance of memory, both collective and individual. *Lepanto* has a memorializing quality through which Chesterton wishes to make present the events of the past. He places the rhetorical device of rhyme at the service of the effort to memorialize an important historical event. Like a great many poets before the invention of the printing press, he is concerned with bringing historical events to life for the largest possible audience. Rhyme is also the device most likely to please the ear of the common man. Chesterton refers to the wide appeal of rhyme in the same essay:

> But the simplest way of putting this popular quality is in a single word: it is a song. Rhyme corresponds to a melody so simple that it goes strait like an arrow to the heart. It corresponds to a chorus so familiar and obvious that all men can join in it. . . . Rhyme is consonant to the particular kind of song that can be a popular song, whether pathetic or

passionate or comic; and Milton is entitled to his true distinction; nobody is likely to sing *Paradise Lost* as if it were a song of that kind.[44]

Chesterton is in one sense a popularizer of history. He thinks that it is important for the common man to be not only aware of his history, but also touched by its colorful details. Every alliterative and rhyming line has a direct appeal to the ear of the common man just as the vibrant descriptions appeal to the eye. A good indicator of Chesterton's success in this area was that the troops shouted lines of *Lepanto* to each other in the trenches of World War I:

> Amid all the praise of his literary peers, perhaps the tribute that pleased Chesterton more than any other was a short note from a soldier named John Buchan which was dated June 21, 1915: 'The other day in the trenches we shouted your *Lepanto*.' [45]

The appeal of the poem for these soldiers of the Great War is a sign that Chesterton's approach to history found a receptive audience among men outside the narrow confines of the academic world. Chesterton was not dismissive of the vivid realities that make history interesting and exciting. Unlike some academic historians, he thought that the truth of the historical events was not lessened in any way by being described in a dramatic fashion. It is clear that Chesterton sides with the forces of Europe, but this does not undermine his factual reporting of the event. He manages to combine a great deal of detailed facts with evocative description and a strong rhythm. One example of this is his account of King Philip of Spain, who collected dwarfs.

> King Philip's in his closet with a fleece about his neck,
> *(Don John of Austria is armed upon the deck.)*
> The walls are hung with velvet that is black and soft as sin,
> And little dwarfs creep out of it and little dwarfs creep in.[46]

The colorful fact that Philip II of Spain collected dwarfs is something that conveys the often frivolous and self-indulgent behavior of those who hold great power. But instead of writing an essay about the dissipating effects of wealth and power, Chesterton conveys much more in these few factual and colorful lines. He is aware of one of the most potent effects of poetry, namely its ability to say more than one thing at a time. Because poetry works on the levels of symbolism, sound, rhythm, imagery and metaphor, it is a fit vehicle to transmit a living sense of history in a way that discursive prose cannot. This reality has been formally recognized by such institutional awards as the Parkman Prize, which is granted in the United States.

Chesterton's poem reaches its climax when the pope is in his chapel and sees a vision of the battle and its resolution. This underlines Chesterton's belief that providence, and not fate, is at work in history. He concludes that God responds to man's requests, and works with man when He is asked for help in benevolent endeavors. Thus, the relationship is one of cooperation rather than one of preordained ends to which man can only bow. History is contingent on the interaction between the will of man and the providence of God. The pope's vision of the battle's outcome ties together the active participation of those fighting in the battle with the divine intervention guiding the outcome.

The stress that Chesterton lays on the role of divine providence removes his view of history from the merely synchronic and broadens it to a concern with the future. This concern touches on Chesterton's understanding of the uses of history. For him, history is not only to be considered as a recital of past events, no matter how stirring, but even more importantly, an impetus to inspire future action. People living in his own time took inspiration from his depiction of past events, and his successful portrayal and effective imagery resulted in people such as the World War I soldiers feeling that they could relate in a very personal way to those who had fought a battle centuries earlier.

In this regard, it is significant that Chesterton ends *Lepanto* with a picture of Cervantes sheathing his sword and entertaining thoughts of his literary creation, Don Quixote. Although Cervantes was wounded three times in the battle, and remained more proud of his participation at Lepanto than of any other accomplishment in his life, he went home to Spain and poured his experience of humanity into his famous novel. Like Chesterton, he had a belief in the teaching power of history and past experience. To have participated in great and pivotal events is not only something to be proud of, but also something to pass on because it gives meaning to the future. Without the reference points of this tradition, those who come later would have difficulty in fitting themselves into the story of history.

> Cervantes on his galley sets the sword back in the sheath
> *(Don John of Austria rides homeward with the wreath.)*
> And he sees across a weary land a straggling road in Spain,
> Upon which a lean and foolish knight forever rides in vain,
> And he smiles, but not as Sultans smile, and settles back the blade -
> *(But Don John of Austria rides home from the Crusade.)*[47]

Like Alfred in *The Ballad of the White Horse*, Cervantes' cheerful optimism ("He smiles, but not as Sultans smile") contrasts with the arrogant, presumptive smile of his enemy. In emphasizing the childlike abandon of Alfred and Cervantes, Chesterton hopes to convey the sense in which Christianity combines the paradoxical elements of putting forth one's best effort while not being overly concerned with the ultimate outcome, trusting that the final page of the story will be written by one who is both omniscient and omnipotent.

If the public and oral quality of Chesterton's ballads was well suited for the description of great events in the external history of a nation, the novel form is more appropriate for the exploration of the interior states of human beings. The form of the novel is discursive and private, and is meant to be enjoyed individually. Chesterton makes use of this form in *The Man Who Was Thursday* to present two rival poets, Lucian Gregory and Gabriel Syme. Gregory is the representative of the aesthetic poet who feels himself to be outside the bounds of law and morality. For him, the only true artist is the one who openly flouts all traditional moral restraints, including those imposed by art. It is not hard to see Chesterton's vision of the aesthetes of the 1890's behind the character of Gregory. In contrast to him is the figure of Gabriel Syme, who is the poet of law and order. Syme rejoices in the world as it is given to him, having only admiration for the beauty and order around him.

The novel begins with an argument between the two men as to which of their respective worldviews is the right one. Gregory sums up his philosophy of life in the following way:

> An artist is identical with an anarchist," he cried. "You might transpose the words anywhere. An anarchist is an artist. The man who throws a bomb is an artist, because he prefers a great moment to everything. He sees how much more valuable is one burst of blazing light, one peal of perfect thunder, than the mere common bodies of a few shapeless policemen. An artist disregards all governments, abolishes all conventions. The poet delights in disorder only. If it were not so, the most poetical thing in the world would be the Underground Railway.[48]

For Gregory, the patient and steady application of the maker and the builder is to be scorned in favor of one large destructive act. He seems to be saying that to strike a great blow against order is a finer way of asserting oneself than quietly creating something beautiful. Syme answers this challenge by pointing out the hidden wonder in the very example used by his antagonist. The underground railway train is wonderful because it always hits its mark and arrives at the correct station. In a chaotic world such as Gregory envisions, the railway might go anywhere.[49]

Syme appreciates the integrated variety that is all around him, but Gregory wants to overturn it without substituting anything else in its place. Gregory does not see the Divine Artist behind beauty in the world. He is a revolutionary without a program to be implemented when the revolution ends. As a character, he embodies the attitude that Chesterton explored in a more abstract way in his book, *Orthodoxy*. In this latter book, Chesterton outlines the degradation that had taken place in European thought since the French revolution.

> But since then the revolutionary or speculative mind of Europe has been weakened by shrinking from any proposal because of the limits of

that proposal. Liberalism has been degraded into liberality. Men have tried to turn 'revolutionize' from a transitive to an intransitive verb.[50]

Before this change took place, it was common for the advocates of revolution to overturn the reigning order so that they could replace it with one more just or more favorable. This goal is what gave the revolutionaries their drive and legitimacy. In the eyes of all who witnessed the revolution, there was some sense that a battle was being waged between two creative forces. Both forces wanted to make something that would have permanent value, even if they disagreed over what that permanent end was. After the revolution, the revolutionaries themselves would become the new regime and cease to have any interest in promoting further revolution. Chesterton's notion of revolutionizing as being an intransitive verb is a grammatical metaphor of a general refusal to accept limits. His emphasis on the unfolding of human capacities in a specific location shows the importance of accepting limits and even celebrating them. Just as Alfred accepts the limited job of governing a small part of Wessex and rejects a wide hegemony after conquering the Danes, or Don John of Austria rides home from the crusade rather than staying behind to expand on his victory, the emphasis is on the creation of something finite and specific over the imperialist extension of raw power without any fruitful program of development.

Lucian Gregory affirms that "the poet is always in revolt."[51] In the two characters, then, Chesterton establishes the opposition between nihilism and the creative participation in the goods that one has been given. The central episodes of the book are framed on either end by the conversation between the two poets. What happens in between has the quality of a dream, a point alluded to in the subtitle of the book, "A Nightmare." Syme goes out into the evening and is taken by Gregory to an anarchist's den where he meets the inner council of the anarchist's society. Each council member is named after a day of the week, *Thursday* having died, and the meeting being called to elect his replacement. Syme reveals to Gregory that he is a policeman, and before Gregory can take action against him, the other conspirators arrive for the election.

Knowing that Syme is a detective, Gregory delivers a speech before his colleagues to gain the empty seat, making light of their anarchic position with the hope of convincing Syme that their intentions are not seriously criminal. His efforts succeed better than he had hoped, ironically resulting in his failure to gain the vacant spot on the council after Syme delivers a fiery speech in favor of anarchy and wins the spot himself. To further the irony, when Gregory protests that Syme is unfit, the other council members silence him.

In this scene, Chesterton shows the contingency of human events. Despite being in a circumscribed situation where he feels in control of all factors, Gregory finds that the outcome of his efforts cannot be fully predicted. His attempts to marginalize the infiltrating detective end up bringing the policeman into the very heart of the secret organization. The theme of making a concentrated effort to effect an outcome and not being so attached to the outcome that another cannot be accepted, seems to apply both to the well-intentioned and creative as well as to the self-serving and destructive as part of the limitation of being a creature subject to wills other than one's own. By virtue of their limitation, Chesterton seems to say, all human actors in history are participants in the superior purview of providence.

For Chesterton, human nature is the limiting factor on all human institutions. Syme is not a detective out of any great tradition of policemen in his family, nor is his profession the fruit of some great primordial love of order and the majesty of the law. Rather, his motivation is that in seeing all the rebellion around him, he rebels.

> Hence the child, during his tender years was wholly unacquainted with any drink between the extremes of Absinthe and cocoa, of both of which he had a healthy dislike. The more his mother preached a more than puritan abstinence the more did his father expand into a more than pagan latitude; by the time the former had come to enforcing vegetarianism, the latter had pretty well reached the point of defending cannibalism.
>
> Being surrounding with every conceivable kind of revolt from infancy, Gabriel had to revolt into something, so he revolted into the only thing left—sanity.[52]

Growing up in this type of environment, Syme's character had been tempered in such a way that he saw the established authorities as the romantic outpost of order standing against a multitude of anarchic foes. This made him want to defend the government and consequently he found common cause with the police force. An instinct to defend the small and weak against the great and powerful is something that Chesterton seems to place at the heart of human nature. Examined from a philosophical standpoint, this sympathy for small things may be understood as the necessary result of the creatureliness of persons. Whether looked at through the lens of duration, knowledge, extension of will, or even physical presence, most humans experience at some time a sense of smallness and limitation.

The next meeting of the anarchist council gives Syme the opportunity to assess the characters of his colleagues. He finds them to be marginal figures who have taken a particular line of thought and followed it to an extreme position. Most puzzling of all is the leader of the council, a gigantic figure named Sunday, whose enigmatic glance stays fixed on Syme, making the detective uncomfortably aware of his deception. When Sunday suddenly announces that there is a spy among them, Syme is ready to react quickly. However, he is shocked to learn that it is a different member, Gogol, who is discovered to be a policeman. This revelation is the first among many others for Syme. He goes on to discover that all of his co-conspirators are in fact members of the police force, each one having infiltrated the council hoping to undermine its nihilistic goals. Syme also discovers that each of the detectives looks at their leader, Sunday, through his own particular philosophical lens.

The theme of limitation is pursued here as it relates to the understanding of each conspirator. Sunday's knowledge seems all-encompassing while each anarchist is shown to be uneasy with only part of the whole picture. As the story unfolds and the particular limitations of the other members become apparent, the figure of Sunday takes on the quality of a symbol. He is more different than anyone can fathom, but he is similar enough to be at least partially knowable by his finite followers. In this respect, his character highlights the human attraction for limitation and specificity that sets the creature off from the infinite transcendence of the creator. When the chase finally ends at Sunday's palatial country estate, Syme, who is Thursday, is attired in a robe emblazoned with the sun and the moon. The symbolism conveys the human desire for limitation, as Chesterton makes clear: "The philosopher may sometimes love the infinite; the poet always loves the finite. For him the great moment is not the creation of light, but the creation of the sun and the moon."[53]

Attempts to foil the anarchists' plot to kill the Russian Tsar and the French president, together with the revelation that the chosen assassin is also a member of the police force, lead all of the conspirators to conclude that the most pressing question is the identity of their leader, Sunday. This development is in keeping with the overall atmosphere of the novel that is one of ambiguity and briefly glimpsed partial truths. For instance, the members of the anarchist group often see only the back of Sunday, or if they do see his front, they find it too large to take in. Sunday represents created nature, in that it is too big to conceive in its entirety, being only partially understood according to the background, beliefs and experience of the perceiver. As in the earlier example of the rationalist who tries to fit the heavens into his head as opposed to the poet who tries to raise his head to the heavens, Chesterton approaches the finite quality of man's mind and contrasts it with the depth of creation. He suggests that one way to approach a subject as great as the created order is to have a variety of people give their own descriptions as they fumble to the gradual conclusion that no one can see the whole picture on his own.

When all six of the detectives set off to discover the truth about the identity of their leader, they are led on a long chase through London and the countryside surrounding the city. Sunday leaves a trail of enigmatic messages for each of his followers, which infuriate them and incite them to redouble their efforts to catch him. When they finally arrive at the end of their pursuit, they are invited into an elaborate garden party at Sunday's country estate. Each has been provided with a throne from which to preside over the party, with Sunday being seated in the center.

Chesterton uses this imagery to suggest that they are the six days of creation, and that Sunday is the final one. Furthermore, the pursuit of the six days has filled them with a burning desire to ask questions, but being in Sunday's presence they fall silent and simply watch the beautiful party as it unfolds before them. All the participants are happily dancing, eating, and drinking in the lovely surroundings, taking little heed of the seven figures seated on the thrones. This scenario suggests that the predominant viewpoint of each of the six days, whether the outlook is materialist, idealist or rationalist, are all somehow preceded by mute wonder.

Chesterton suggests that all the characters of the days are both innocent and guilty: They are both patriots and rebels who want to preserve and take care of the order of things. The rebellion comes from a primordial rupture known as original sin. When Syme is recruited into the police force, the constable in charge explains to him that there are two levels to the anarchic movement. The outer ring is the innocent section consisting of those who believe that rules and formulas have destroyed human happiness and need to be abolished. The inner ring consists of the supremely guilty few. The constable explains:

> 'They also speak to applauding crowds of the happiness of the future, and of mankind freed at last. But in their mouths'—and the policeman lowered his voice—'these happy phrases have a horrible meaning. They are under no illusions; they are too intellectual to think that man upon this earth can ever be quite free of original sin and the struggle. And they mean death. When they say that mankind shall be free at last, they mean that mankind shall commit suicide. When they talk of a paradise without right or wrong, they mean the grave. They have but two objects, to destroy first humanity and then themselves.' [54]

Chesterton uses this as an expression of the importance of accepting the given conditions that are found in the created order rather than trying to create conditions anew. The anarchist-policemen are ultimately not able to understand all that has befallen them, but they are given a chance to accept the gratuity of creation and then affirm it. The history of their world is too complex to be completely fathomed but it is wonderful enough to hold their interest and elicit their participation.

At the end of the book, when all the men come before Sunday and give him various statements regarding their lack of understanding of him, Sunday says nothing but points to a new arrival who has come to complain. The newcomer is Lucian Gregory who asserts that if he could, he would destroy the world. He says that what he has against the seven figures seated on the thrones is that they have not suffered, which is to say that they have never given of themselves but only received.

Syme responds that they have also given up something, if only the disordered desire to be more than the recipient of gifts that they do not comprehend. Despite the fact that they did not understand the gifts, they have looked for answers and eventually recognized the value of the gifts, and sought to protect them while coming to a greater, albeit not exhaustive, understanding of them.

> Syme sprang to his feet shaking from head to foot. 'I see everything,' he cried, 'everything that there is. Why does each thing on the earth war against each other thing? Why does each small thing in the world have to fight against the world itself? Why does a fly have to fight the whole universe? Why does a dandelion have to fight the whole universe? For the same reason that I had to be alone in the dreadful council of the days so that each thing that obeys law may have the glory and isolation of the anarchist. So that each man fighting for order may be as brave and good a man as the dynamiter.[55]

Like Adam Wayne, Syme understands that by struggling to affirm what is good in created order, a creature will only deepen his love and appreciation for the specific locality that he has been given him. Chesterton implies that the foundation of thinking about the world is a fundamental acceptance of the given nature of the created order. This is what Lucian Gregory does not do, but instead he rebels against it. Each of the six days has something of the rebel in him, but also something of the patriot. Each one is a policeman who wants to protect the given order of things and a rebel who chafes under the aspects of creation that clash with his particular temperamental disposition toward reality. For instance, one of the weak points of the artistic temperament is that, while it is sensitive to the beauty in creation, it is insensitive to the goodness of creation when it threatens to obscure the artistic fixation on beauty. Poets can hate noisy, meddlesome, inconvenient and willful humanity while professing to love the structures and patterns found in nature.

The story is concluded when Lucian Gregory and Gabriel Syme find themselves walking again in the garden in Saffron Park where their original argument began. All of the wild incidents of the story are thus placed in the context of a nightmarish dream that is the fitting context for the elaboration of such fluid states as the interior dispositions of the characters. *The Man Who Was Thursday* elaborates on an aspect of Chesterton's philosophy of history that is most concerned with interior dispositions of the human being. Unlike *The Ballad of the White Horse* and *Lepanto* which deal more with external events, *The Man Who Was Thursday* explores the interior landscape of the human story, and attempts to delineate fundamental approaches to created reality that precede and condition historical action. Guthrum's nihilism as well as the Sultan of Byzantium's arrogant fatalism need to be understood as mysterious choices made in the internal dialogue between rebel and patriot that occurs within each person.

5 The Critical and Creative Legacy
Dawson, Waugh, and McLuhan

Despite spending most of his working life as a journalist, Chesterton was decidedly different from the bulk of journalistic writers in the deep influence that he exerted on writers and thinkers who outlived him. Perhaps one reason for this is that, while Chesterton often dealt with contemporary ephemeral events, he did so in such a way that he combined a broad historical perspective with a synchronic attention to structures. He would go into the details of contemporary events without forgetting the context in which these events unfolded. In one sense, Chesterton foreshadowed the Formalist School in his attention to structures without rejecting historical considerations and thereby isolating his conclusions by depriving them of a connection with the past and ultimately, the future. Three examples of Chesterton's ability to influence the outlook of other writers can be found in the historian Christopher Dawson (1889–1970), the novelist Evelyn Waugh (1903–1966), and the critic Marshall McLuhan (1911–1980). As for these and other writers, the legacy of Chesterton's historical thought was fruitful in its effects on thinkers of varying temperaments and interests.

Commenting on Christopher Dawson's early career, his daughter Christina notes his admiration for Chesterton's writing while retaining his own independence of thought.

> In the Catholic Church, Christopher went his own solitary way and was not affiliated to any particular group, neither that of Father Martindale nor of Chesterton and Belloc, who represented the two dominant trends in the 1920's. Christopher admired Chesterton's work and also came to know him later. Belloc he preferred more as a poet than as a historian, for he considered his views one-sided and unreliable, nor did he feel at home with Belloc's particular brand of triumphant Catholicism.[1]

At the time his daughter alludes to, Dawson was making an intensive study of world civilizations in preparation for a five-volume history of culture. The young historian's distaste for Belloc's historical approach indicates his desire to do justice to different points of view and a determination to understand the distinctiveness of different cultures before judging them. Dawson's attitude is reminiscent of Chesterton's approach to history in allowing for the complexity that follows from human freedom. The corruption of the Spanish government during the reign of Philip II is not to be overlooked, but at the same time, Spain's contribution to the Christian victory at Lepanto must be considered. This tendency to see simultaneously both the light and the dark in any historical picture seems to spring from Chesterton's magnanimous disposition, and provided a distinctive difference between Belloc and him.

Chesterton's intuitive and holistic approach to understanding the historical past was a source of inspiration for Dawson when he was deeply immersed in the academic histories of his preparatory studies. Like Chesterton, he came to believe that gaining an understanding of history that went beyond mere factual recitation required a vision inaccessible to the materialist or the rationalist. Unlike Belloc, Dawson could see the good points of those historians whose approach he disagreed with in significant respects. Speaking of her father's approach to some contemporary historians, Christina Scott points out this attribute:

> While he criticized The Decline of the West for its fatalism, its special pleading and forcing of the facts, he later defended Spengler and Toynbee from general attacks on 'metahistory', because he believed that vision, 'partaking more of the nature of religious contemplation than of scientific generalization, was a mainspring of creative power in them as it had been in Toqueville and Ranke.' [2]

This aspect of Dawson's historical approach underscores his belief that a philosophy of history is not only possible but also desirable. Such a philosophy provides the framework within which to understand the relative significance of past events. This regard for a unifying vision provided the inspiration for one of Dawson's most important works, *The Making of Europe,* subtitled *An Introduction to the History of European Unity.* In this work, Dawson tries to show that Europe is an organic unity that grew out of a common spiritual past. He does not regard this common origin as a cause for rejecting the various national European cultures of his own time, but rather as a powerful aid to understanding and preserving what he considered to be a unique achievement of civilization.

Dawson was able to encourage appreciation of national identities, while simultaneously advocating, at least on one level, the transcendence of culture.

> The evil of nationalism does not consist in its loyalty to the traditions of the past or in its vindication of national unity and the right of self-determination. What is wrong is the identification of this unity with the ultimate and inclusive unity of culture which is a supernatural thing.

> The ultimate foundation of our culture is not the national state, but the European unity. It is true that this unity has not hitherto achieved political form, and perhaps it may never do so; but for all that it is a real society, not an intellectual abstraction, and it is only through their communion in that society that the different national cultures have attained their actual form.³

Like Chesterton, Dawson was careful to balance the claims of a national culture with a true regard for where that culture originated. The locality that lends the particular color and variety to each culture does not exhaust the meaning of that culture, but gives specific form to a content that transcends national boundaries. Dawson would agree with Chesterton's understanding of patriotism as love of one's own origins that could be balanced with a healthy aversion to the shortcomings of one's nation. Chesterton gives an example of his understanding of patriotism that might seem absurd to a proponent of a kind of nationalism that Dawson criticizes. In *The New Jerusalem*, Chesterton speaks to the English influence in the Mideast:

> The position of the English in Egypt or even in Palestine is something of a paradox. We do indeed hear a number of false English claims, and other English claims that are rather irrelevant than false. We hear pompous and hypocritical suggestions, full of that which so often accompanies the sin of pride, the weakness of provinciality. We hear suggestions that the English alone can establish anywhere a reign of law, justice, mercy, purity and all the rest of it.⁴

Chesterton and Dawson share an awareness of the human frailty held by the peoples of different nations that is a result of their common humanity. They do not lose sight of this simple truth when they consider the raw material and the various components out of which Europe was constructed.

In speaking of Dawson's work on *The Making of Europe*, his biographer singles out four pillars that he designated as foundations of the cultures of the various European nations:

> The foundations on which he considered European unity had been built were four: the Roman Empire, the Christian Church, the classical tradition, and finally the barbarian societies. All of these factors had contributed something, whether political, spiritual or intellectual to the commonwealth of Europe. The barbarians, he said 'provided the human material out of which Europe has been fashioned: they are the gentes against the imperium and the ecclesia—the source of the national element in European life.'⁵

The delineation of these categories immediately brings to mind Chesterton's representative characterization of Alfred's allies in *The Ballad of the*

White Horse: Mark the Roman, Colan the Celt and Eldred the Saxon joining with Alfred the Christian king to oppose the destructive nihilism of the invading Danes. Chesterton's characters give imaginative color and weight to the historical influences that Dawson emphasizes.

In the relatively short space of his poem, Chesterton manages to convey a unified story that vividly impresses on the reader events and influences that unfolded over a period of many centuries in the actual history of Europe in general, and England in particular. In his preface to *The Ballad of the White Horse*, Chesterton makes explicit the effect that his poem achieves. He states, " . . . it is the chief value of legend to mix up the centuries while preserving the sentiment; to see all ages in a sort of splendid foreshortening. That is the use of tradition: it telescopes history."[6] In his achievement in writing the *Ballad of the White Horse*, Chesterton was following in the footsteps of one of the Western tradition's most influential literary figures, the Roman writer Virgil.[7]

Chesterton's achievement was not lost on the poem's admirers, prominent among them being the young Christopher Dawson. After completing his work on *The Making of Europe* in 1932, Dawson sent a copy to Chesterton with the following letter:

> Years ago when I was an undergraduate your Ballad of the White Horse first brought the breath of life to this period for me when I was fed up with Stubbs and Oman and the rest of them. Unfortunately, the boredom that is generated in people's minds by academic history leads to a positive anti-historicism which seems to me becoming characteristic of modern 'left-wing' thought. I have tried to write a history that does not leave out everything that matters, in the academic fashion, and that gives a proper place to spiritual factors. Unfortunately I am afraid that my book is in danger of falling between two stools—being too popular for the academic public and too abstruse for the general reader.[8]

In contrasting Chesterton's historical vision with that of a historian such as Stubbs, Dawson clarifies a particular point of difference between his immediate predecessors and himself. William Stubbs was the Regius Professor of history at Oxford from 1866–1901 and was responsible for editing a large number of original documents in English constitutional history. Dawson's own historical writings reflected a similar preoccupation with primary sources and detail, but departed from his academic forbearers in his desire to reach a wider audience, but perhaps more importantly, exert an influence on the construction of a better future for the English nation. Dawson saw history as a living instrument whereby humanity might benefit, and not just as an academic exercise.

In taking pains to give full expression to the spiritual forces at work in history, Dawson shows himself to be a historian of ideas to the same degree as Chesterton, albeit in a more formal sense of the term. The following example serves to illustrate the way in which Dawson attached the greatest importance to the spiritual relationships that gave meaningful structure to human history:

> In every aspect of the later medieval culture we find this conception of a hierarchy of goods and values and a corresponding hierarchy of estates and vocations which bind the whole range of human relations together in an ordered spiritual structure that reaches from earth to heaven. Nevertheless the completeness and symmetry of the Thomist synthesis should not blind us to the fact that it rests on a very delicate balance of opposing forces and different traditions which can only be maintained by a strict adherence to an order of ethical and metaphysical requirements that rests in the last resort upon an act of faith.[9]

Dawson highlights the spiritual hierarchy that underpinned the medieval synthesis much in the same way as Chesterton did. As outlined in Chapter Three, Chesterton stresses the potential tension between pagan antiquity and Christian belief, and points to the medieval synthesis of these two spiritual realities as one of its most characteristic features. This ability of Christianity to absorb, appropriate and synthesize elements as disparate as barbarian and classical elements is a note that both Chesterton and Dawson develop at some length in their historical writings regarding Europe. They both regard Christianity as human enough to resonate with whatever is human, and supernatural enough to provide a glue that transcends the specific differences of localities. As Chesterton says in the *Ballad of the White Horse*, " . . . it is only Christian men [who] guard even heathen things." [10]

Chesterton and Dawson's similar insistence on the primacy of religion as the foundation of culture will sometimes result in striking parallels in their writing. In his introduction to *The Making of Europe*, Dawson remarks on a possible difficulty that might be encountered by a non- Christian reader:

> . . . if the non-religious reader should feel that an undue amount of space or of emphasis has been given in this book to theological or ecclesiastical matters, he must remember that it is impossible to understand the past unless we understand the things for which the men of the past cared most. The very fact that these things are still matters of interest to theologians is apt to lead to their neglect by the historians, with the result that the latter devote more space to secondary movements that make some appeal to the modern mind than to the central issues that were of vital interest to the men of the past and governed not only their inner life but also their social institutions and their practical activities.[11]

It is instructive to compare this with the following passage from Chesterton's *A Short History of England*. Speaking of Alfred's victory over Guthrum the Dane, Chesterton says:

Guthrum was baptized, and the Treaty of Wedmore secured the clearance of Wessex. The modern reader will smile at the baptism, and turn with greater interest to the terms of the treaty. In this acute attitude the modern reader will be vitally and hopelessly wrong. He must support the tedium of frequent references to the religious element in this part of English history, for without it there would never have been any English history at all. And nothing could clinch this truth more than the case of the Danes. In all the facts that followed, the baptism of Guthrum is really much more important than the Treaty of Wedmore. The treaty itself was a compromise, and even as such it did not endure; a century afterwards a Danish king like Canute was really ruling in England. But though the Dane got the crown, he did not get rid of the cross. It was precisely Alfred's religious exaction that remained unalterable.[12]

Like Dawson, Chesterton was consistently aware of the enduring elements in the historical past that provided continuity amidst ongoing complexity and change. While human nature was one of the continuous elements, an equally significant place was accorded to the spiritual realities. In his own way, the novelist Evelyn Waugh attached prime importance to the influence of the spiritual in history. Although writing as a member of the generation that followed Chesterton, Waugh was an admirer of Chesterton's specifically historical work. Like Chesterton, he was a convert to Roman Catholicism, and both men saw the element of the spiritual as holding the key to history.

The biographer Martin Stannard attests to this viewpoint when discussing Waugh's reaction to the fashionable socialism of his youth:

Waugh was appalled at the socialist/humanist view of history. He saw no process of inarrestable, beneficial change nor a legacy of exploitation. Human suffering, he thought, was constant whatever the government or material circumstances of the individual: it was a spiritual, not a material question.[13]

Waugh's skepticism concerning a one-directional progressive path of improvement in history places him in line with Chesterton, and indicates his belief that history is written by the interplay between human nature and both material and spiritual factors that reoccur with every generation. This philosophy of an unchanging human nature coupled with a belief in the primacy of spiritual factors and the decisive part played by human freedom gives Waugh a place to stand when judging the past.

By temperament, Waugh was inclined to be austere in his judgments and exacting in his compliments. The confidence that he felt in his philosophy was supported by the age-long experience of the church that he entered as a young man, and the keen critical intelligence that he had developed in his classical education. When he turned this intelligence to the appraisal of other nations and cultures, he made short work of those who did not anchor themselves in the truths that had been proven by centuries of tradition.

An example of this can be seen in his reaction to the customs he encountered on a visit to southern California, which he summarized in a magazine article that he published in 1947, and which later formed the basis of his satirical novel, *The Loved One*. After visiting the celebrity, Las Vegas-style cemetery of Forest Lawn in Los Angeles, he conjectured about the reaction of future archeologists when they would come upon the ruins of such an establishment with all that it would have to say about a people's approach to the pivotal reality of death. Taking such an artifact at face value, they would naturally come to conclusions at variance with the whole tradition of Western civilization informed by the classical thinkers and Christians of a life after death in which punishment for evil and reward for good would be meted out. The whole framework of Chaucer's pilgrims is summarily lost because at Forest Lawn there is neither the doctrine of Purgatory nor the earthly works and prayers that might gain some remission of the punishment due to sin. Milton and Shakespeare lose significance because Hamlet's father is no longer in need of being put to rest and Lucifer has never left paradise. Waugh sees the California cemetery as an example of what absurdity lies in wait for those who have neither tradition nor a philosophy of man with which to look at the past. Projecting the reader into a future 1000 years hence, Waugh elaborates on the conjectures of future historians who will operate without the benefit of a coherent philosophy:

> What will the archeologist of 2947 make of all this and of the countless other rarities of the place? What webs of conjecture will be spun by the professors of comparative religion? We know with what confidence they define the intimate beliefs of remote ages. They flourished in the nineteenth century. Then G.K. Chesterton in a masterly book, sadly neglected in Europe but honored in the U.S.A.—The Everlasting Man—gently exposed their fatuity. [14]

Waugh's admiration for Chesterton's *The Everlasting Man* is significant not only because he was parsimonious in his praise of other writers, but also because the historical philosophy expressed by Chesterton is clearly laid out in the work. Its influence on Waugh was decisive[15] and, like Chesterton, Waugh's tendency was toward an artistic and aesthetic expression of his views. In this respect, it is not surprising that a colorful, aesthetic monstrosity such as Forest Lawn evoked such a strong reaction in Waugh.

Waugh was no writer of dry historical treatises as was confirmed by his experience in writing *Edmund Campion*. Most of the detailed historical research for that book was done by someone else who had the misfortune to die before completing a planned biography of the saint.[16] In fact, Waugh far surpasses Chesterton in his abilities as a novelist and is commonly regarded as a master stylist. The tendency of his analytical mind was to be attracted by the truth or falsity manifested in a particular historical situation. But Waugh framed his evaluation of these situations in highly polished aesthetic form. This tendency of Waugh made him give expression to his historical convictions in a way that was inspired by Chesterton, but departed from the latter's favored form. A novel such as *The Ball and the Cross*, with its allegorical characters standing in for contending philosophical positions, would have been distasteful to a man of Waugh's refined literary sensibilities.

In *Edmund Campion*, Waugh conveys the saint's life as a work of beauty achieved through the influence of grace and the cooperation of free will. Waugh's temperamental attraction to beauty in all its forms is evident when he speaks of Campion's abilities as a writer in his chapter entitled "The Scholar". Citing Campion's work as a student on a book about the history of Ireland, Waugh points out that, had he lived, he would have been one of the great writers of English.

> The History of Ireland is a superb piece of literature comparable in vigor and rhythm to anything written in his day. With all its imperfections of structure and material, it is enough to show that, had Campion continued in the life he was then planning for himself, he would, almost certainly, have come down in history as one of the great masters of English prose.[17]

It is apparent that for Waugh, the avenue toward truth is through beauty. In the end, he realized that the claims of pure aesthetic appreciation had to be subordinated to a higher beauty of the moral order that encompassed the whole of one's life. Like Chesterton, in his own way Waugh had to struggle with an artistic temperament that gravitated toward the beautiful but could easily result in the dismissal of higher claims if they were not integrated. Chesterton struggled with the aesthetic excesses of *fin de siècle* England and emerged with just such an integrated appreciation for the claims of beauty and truth. Waugh came to his own synthesis in this regard as is evidenced by his affirmation of Campion's decisive choice to embrace the whole truth, even to the point of foregoing a promising future in his beloved England. In this respect, Campion exemplifies the patriotism that Chesterton so frequently espoused because he died upholding the good of his country even though his death was at the hands of his fellow countrymen. Waugh contrasts the paradoxical choice of the gifted Campion foregoing a bright future for the sake of a higher ideal, to the bewilderment of Queen Elizabeth and her advisors:

> They had no desire to kill the virtuous and gifted man who had once been their friend, a man, moreover, who could still be of good service to them. From earliest youth, among those nearest them, they had been used to the spectacle of men who would risk their lives for power, but

to die deliberately, without hope of release, for an idea, was something beyond their comprehension.[18]

This theme of the inadequacies of aesthetics alone is similarly explored by Waugh in his novel, *Brideshead Revisited*. The artist, Charles Ryder, resonates to all things beautiful but is a witness to the limitations of such an attitude when it is divorced from a concern for moral truth. The significance of this theme in Waugh's writing is further emphasized by his biographer. Speaking of Waugh's attitude toward the historical trends of his own time, Stannard states the following:

> His developing antagonism towards the obscurities of modernism was based firmly upon the principle that 'ideas . . . demanded communication'. The ideas communicated here were crucial to him. There can be no doubt that Campion was an extremely important book to Waugh—perhaps the first to which he was wholly committed. He looked to it to establish his integrity among intelligent Catholics and it seems, from the biography's polemical nature, that he wanted at last to be accepted into the ranks of the popular apologists: Ronald Knox, G.K. Chesterton and Hilaire Belloc. . . . Waugh's perspective was essentially that of the aesthete, the man who fears the erosion of the artistic developments of Catholic Europe.[19]

What Waugh examined in expository form in the biography of Edmund Campion, he took up again in the novel when he wrote *Brideshead Revisited*. Here he was able to study the life of a lapsed Catholic family viewed through the aesthetic lens of the artist narrator Ryder, who typifies many of Waugh's own attitudes. To Charles Ryder, the Flyte family represents a picture of English Catholic aristocracy in a variety of stages. The faithful mother and daughter, the dutiful but smothered eldest son, the wayward daughter, the profligate youngest son and the absent father who has abandoned his faith to live in Venice with his mistress. With this cast of characters, Waugh is able to do something that Chesterton could not, even though his theme is consonant with Chesterton's historical views.

The story is one of how the workings of Providence are manifest through a variety of human temperaments and choices played out in a concrete historical circumstance, the center of which is the specific locality of Brideshead. None of the characters knows how their choices will affect the ultimate outcome of their family history. However, Waugh's treatment highlights his belief in the primacy of spiritual realities working amidst the complexities of human history. The progress of the Flyte family history is not linear, but follows instead an unpredictable path of fortune and misfortune that Charles Ryder eventually comes to see as unified only by an overarching spiritual reality. Revisiting the Flyte's country house many years after his involvement with the family, Ryder reflects on the unintended consequences of human action:

> Something quite remote from anything the builders intended had come out of their work, and out of the fierce little human tragedy in which I played; something none of us thought about at the time: a small red flame—a beaten-copper lamp of deplorable design, re-lit before the beaten-copper doors of a tabernacle; the flame which the old knights saw from their tombs, which they saw put out; that flame burns again for other soldiers, far from home, farther, in heart, than Acre or Jerusalem. It could not have been lit but for the builders and the tragedians, and there I found it this morning, burning anew among the old stones.[20]

In this passage, Waugh expresses in a prose that reflects his aesthetic temperament the theme of a continuity in English history, extending from medieval times and following a winding path into the present. Chesterton's similar preoccupation with the living effect of tradition and the persistence of the transcendent is reworked here in the more private and psychological form of the novel.

For his part, Waugh saw himself as more realistic than Chesterton in his assessment of the depths to which human beings could go in their complicity with evil. Although he greatly admires and even emulates Chesterton's approach to the complexities of history, in this one area Waugh sees Chesterton to be deficient. Speaking of *The Man Who Was Thursday*, Waugh considers the story to be naïve, with its sinister conspirators all revealed as policemen and the mysterious Sunday as the "beaming, tutelary, Cheeryble Brother, god of the hearth".[21] Here Waugh shows an inability to see any greater depth in Chesterton's novel, and seems to ignore the attention given by Chesterton to the place of evil in human affairs. For instance, the character of Lucian Gregory is a destroyer on a grand scale, and Sunday has suffered much before he takes his place as the host of the party. Writing his critique of the novel in 1947, Waugh was careful to point out that the events of the previous decade showed an evil that would find no place in Chesterton's world. Referring to his arguably simplistic reading of *The Man Who Was Thursday*, Waugh says the following:

> Could Chesterton have written like that today, if he had lived to see the Common Man in arms, drab, grey and brown, the Storm Troopers and the Partisans, standard-bearers of the great popular movements of the century; Had he lived to read in the evidence of the War Trials the sickening accumulation of brutality inflicted and condoned by common men, and seen, impassive on the bench, the agents of other criminals, vile, but free and triumphant? Chesterton was the poetic and romantic child of a smug tradition.[22]

Waugh's analysis has something in common with critics who confuse Chesterton's amiability and good nature with a lack of depth when it comes to the understanding of the gravity and ubiquity of original sin. Waugh's judgment in this particular area is countered by another writer of his generation, the Canadian teacher and critic, Marshall McLuhan. Writing in 1936, McLuhan made his academic publishing debut with an article entitled, "G.K. Chesterton: A Practical Mystic". In it he observes the following:

> Chesterton himself is full of that childlike surprise and enjoyment which a sophisticated age supposes to be able to exist only in children. And it is to this more than ordinary awareness and freshness of perception that we may attribute his extraordinarily strong sense of fact.[23]

Waugh's sophistication prevented him from understanding that Chesterton could combine childlike wonder at every variety of existence without becoming childish in his awareness of the rejection of existence that constituted evil.

McLuhan first encountered Chesterton as an undergraduate and immediately responded to his distinctive way of looking at the world. In 1931, McLuhan was in his third year of studies at the University of Manitoba. After reading *What's Wrong With the World,* he recorded his reaction in his diary:

> It seems to me that G.K.'s words are most valuable when he hangs them on some subject that would seem to admit of no extraneous discussion. No matter what, G.K. had [something] to say on any subject however irrelevant in such a manner as to make the connection at once obvious and important. Few writers, yes I can say, no other writer has ever before been able to arouse my enthusiasm for ideas as has G.K.[24]

Chesterton's habit of finding paradox appealed to McLuhan because his own wide reading and sense of intellectual adventure encouraged him to see the world in a similar way. Growing up on the Canadian prairie near what was then the frontier town of Edmonton, McLuhan was in close contact with nature. This proximity piqued his interest and developed his powers of observation. He became an avid sailor and at one point built a sailboat to use on the nearby Red River. When he encountered Chesterton's writing, he was predisposed to resonate to the Englishman's keen interest in the world around him. Chesterton's readiness to try out new ideas in a playful way while remaining anchored in reason was just the combination that McLuhan found in himself.[25]

After arriving in Cambridge, England in 1934 to continue his studies, McLuhan had the opportunity to hear Chesterton speak to the Distributist League. His biographer recounts how later in his life McLuhan was to remember the impression that Chesterton made on him:

Nearly forty years later, McLuhan said: 'I know every word of him: he's responsible for bringing me into the church. He writes by paradox—that makes him hard to read (or hard on the reader).' Chesterton and St. Thomas Aquinas he said, were his two biggest influences. He loved Chesterton's rhetorical flourishes, imbibed his playfulness, turned his impulse to try out new combinations of ideas into the hallmark of the McLuhan method.[26]

Having grown up a Baptist, McLuhan was well-versed in the Bible, but his exposure to Chesterton and Aquinas watered the seeds of his philosophical temperament so that he was encouraged to integrate the natural and the supernatural, the material and the spiritual. McLuhan saw Chesterton's paradoxical approach to reality as the only way in which things could be looked at simultaneously under different aspects. Already by temperament inclined to reject any sort of reductionism, McLuhan's encounter with Chesterton opened new doors for him in his attempts to do justice to the vast body of literature and history that interested him.[27]

McLuhan recognized that his capacity for enthusiasm might incline him to focus on a particular truth and not relate it to others. Chesterton located truth in this very fact of relationship using his paradoxical approach to avoid leaving any truth unrelated to another. When McLuhan encountered I.A. Richards at Cambridge, he was repulsed by his atheism but attracted to the analytical tools of formalism that Richards was teaching to his students. Richards' attention to exploring the structural relationships of poetry and prose found an enthusiastic disciple in McLuhan.[28] But whereas Richards's approach was self-contained and not related to any transcendent order, Chesterton combined the advantages of Richards's attention to structural details with a wider vision of how those details fit into a metaphysical reality that put art in its proper place without diminishing more all-encompassing realities.

In effect, Chesterton gave McLuhan a philosophy and a method that would allow him to deal with both the general and the specific, whereas Richards dealt with the specific but failed to place it in a meaningful context, hoping to find in art an ultimate truth. Another way in which McLuhan departed from Richards's influence was in his desire to gain a greater historical understanding as opposed to remaining at the synchronic level. Here again he found Chesterton to be a model for the integration of multiple points of view. McLuhan describes this particular ability of Chesterton in his essay, "Chesterton: A Practical Mystic":

> What Chesterton has written of the power of St. Thomas to fix even passing things as they pass, and to scorch details under the magnifying lens of his attention, is strikingly true of himself. His is the power to focus a vast range of material into narrow compass; and his books though very numerous are extremely condensed. They might even be considered as projections of his mastery of epigram and sententious

phrase. What had seemed a dull and formless expanse of history is made to shine with contemporary significance, and contemporary details are made to bristle with meaning. It is a great labor of synthesis and reconstruction in which Chesterton has been engaged. He has fixed his attention on the present and the past, because he is concerned lest our future steps be blindly mistaken.[29]

In his doctoral thesis at Cambridge, McLuhan covered a wide historical period beginning with the pre-Socratic authors and ending with the Renaissance. In his thesis, he explored the roles of logic and analogy as ways of understanding the world. He claimed to have found a pattern whereby these two approaches competed with each other for predominance, and depending on which one was most favored at a given time, that particular period in history would take on a distinctive coloration. By temperament and talent, McLuhan himself was more sympathetic to an analogical method of thought. He finds this method widely employed in Chesterton's writing when he identifies the latter's ability to look at things not so much in a linear discursive way, but rather in an artistic comparative way.

McLuhan was of the opinion that since the advent of literacy and mass circulation of print, the linear logical way of looking at the world, encouraged by the very act of writing, had come to influence modes of thought so strongly that the fruitful method of analogical thinking was all but lost. As a result, reality and specifically, historical reality, were no longer adequately understood because, by their very nature, they required an approach that was congruent with their simultaneity and complexity. From his insight into the direct effect of literacy on man's way of thinking, McLuhan was able to draw his later principle of the "medium is the message": The way in which something is done changes and limits its perceptive outcomes. [30]

In his 1948 essay entitled "Where Chesterton Comes In," McLuhan was able to state precisely this method whereby Chesterton eschewed linear dialectical thinking in favor of analogical thought:

> The specific contemporary relevance of Chesterton is this, that his metaphysical intuition of being was always in the service of the search for moral and political order in the current chaos. He was a Thomist by connaturality with being, not by study of St. Thomas. And unlike the neo-Thomists his unfailing sense of the relevance of the analogy of being directed his intellectual gaze not to the schoolman but to the heart of the chaos of our time. . . . He seems never to have reached any position by dialectic or doctrine but to have enjoyed a kind of connaturality with every kind of reasonableness.[31]

Chesterton's concern to relate the historical past to the unrealized future of his country was an aspect of his thought that McLuhan understood to be related to his patriotism. McLuhan recognized that Chesterton's patriotism was rooted in a desire to retain the best principles of the past and integrate them with the realities of the present. Like Chesterton, McLuhan saw the path of history as one which was indirect and circling back, never quite visiting the same place twice but nonetheless, taking all sorts of unpredictable detours as it moved forward. Patriotism was another way of saying that one should not leave the path just because it became steep or seemingly impossible. Instead, Chesterton advocated taking a long look at the path and if necessary, walking back a few miles to retrieve essential equipment that had been foolishly left behind. The rhetorical device of metaphor, even such a pedestrian one as a path, is exactly the device that McLuhan found most useful in understanding the realities of history. Chesterton's reliance on this way of thinking was the mainstay of his patriotic attempts to not only improve his own locality, but also a means whereby he could recognize the strengths of other nations. McLuhan recognizes and approves of this in "G. K. Chesterton: A Practical Mystic":

> But in nothing is the peculiar quality of the autochthonous Englishman seen more clearly than in Chesterton's patriotism. To people unacquainted with the profound patriotism of Sir Thomas More, Johnson, Cobbett and Dickens, it may be puzzling.... The high standard he sets for his own country makes him quick and generous in his recognition of the rights and virtues of others. And the French, American, and Irish peoples have no more discriminating admirer and interpreter than Chesterton. But like Socrates, he is a gadfly stinging his own countrymen into awareness of the crime of complacency.[32]

McLuhan's appreciation for Chesterton's broad philosophical grounding is linked to his approval of Chesterton's patriotism. Precisely because Chesterton was aware of the common elements that united all humanity—a human nature, the effects of the Fall, and an innate tendency to affirm one's locality—he was able to advocate a patriotism that could be encouraged in every country without the danger of a collapse into nationalism.

The influence that Chesterton's historical thought exerted on Dawson, Waugh, and McLuhan is certain evidence of the appeal and power of his ideas. In present-day literary and critical trends there is increasing attention being paid to matters of history and the writing of history. Specifically, this attention focuses on the role of literary art in historical writing and the related question of whether or not historical writing has any claim to truth or objectivity. Since this book aims to show some connections between Chesterton's preoccupation with locality, the centrality of that preoccupation to his philosophy of history, and the expression of this philosophy in literary forms, it makes sense to make some mention of present day scholarship concerned with precisely this topic of history and literary form.

A NOTE ON MODERN HISTORIOGRAPHY

One of the most well-known and influential contemporary scholars writing about historiography is Hayden White. Born in 1928, White came to prominence with the publication of *Metahistory: The Historical Imagination in Nineteenth-Century Europe* (1973). Here he argues that the writing of history involves the more or less conscious use of various literary figures or tropes. The use of these tropes will determine the kind of story that the historian tells. Each writer of history chooses a literary form in which to contain the facts of history and this choice of form is dependent on what the writer wants to convey. Concerning this choice White notes that "commitment to a particular form of knowledge predetermines the kinds of generalization one can make." [33]

These generalizations will be made by the reader when he or she becomes aware that the history under consideration conforms to certain plot types, for example, tragedy or comedy. If the tragic plot is used by the historian, then the reader will infer that the historical events being described are to be interpreted in a serious way with all the reactions characteristic of one who witnesses a tragedy. The reader will be reminded of "the resignations of men to the conditions under which they must labor in the world. These conditions, in turn, are asserted to be unalterable and eternal."[34] Thus, White argues that the writing of history is much more an interpretation than a simple recording or description of objective facts.

In order to make sense of the facts that he or she chooses to examine, the historian is forced to supply connections between them. In the absence of such connective writing, the chosen facts would be a simple list or chronicle with no apparent organizing principle. But, according to White, even in this case the historian has made a choice of some facts over others and this choice in itself is a rudimentary organization based on some previous criteria: "For the chronicle is no less constituted as a record of the past by the historian's own agency than is the narrative which he constructs on its basis."[35]

Having established that the historian must make use of literary forms to embody his historical materials, White points to the inevitability of ideological influence in the writing of history. Since every writer must choose to tell history as a story, it is incumbent on the better historian to let his reader know which tropes he prefers and why. When he is honest with the reader, the historian will reveal, for example, that he has chosen to use a particular trope because it conveys an interpretation of historical events that he finds beautiful or perhaps morally instructive.

White's analysis of the nature of historiography does not stop at showing the historian's ideological bias but locates the tropic forms in consciousness itself. He sees that "history, like other formalizations of poetic insight, was as much a 'making' as it was a 'finding' of the facts that comprised the structure of its perceptions"[36] This assertion has motivated other scholars, such as C. Behan McCullagh, to examine the "truth value" in history in a detailed way.

In his essay, "The Truth of Historical Narratives", McCullagh points out that White's insights have contributed substantially to the understanding of literary forms in historical writing.[37] McCullagh contends, however, that historical writing is not radically incapable of conveying a truth that corresponds to an objective reality independent of categories in the human mind. "In practice we assume that our knowledge of the world correctly represents reality, that it is true in a correspondence sense. We can never prove that this is so; we cannot even prove the truth of our knowledge of the present world, which is supported by perception."[38] McCullagh lays out detailed criteria for judging the objectivity of historical writing and, while conceding it to be a construction, he does not agree with White's understanding of the term as something subjective. The "truth value" of history is similar to our common-sense understanding of truth: "Historical knowledge is but an extension of our everyday knowledge of the past, and should be regarded accordingly."[39] McCullagh's qualified approval of White's insights is but one of many reactions to the pervasive modern tendency to frame philosophies of history in terms of literary technique.[40]

Chesterton's approach to coherence in history is closer to McCullagh regarding the possibility of truth as an objective fact outside the mind. Chesterton's Thomistic worldview has little in common with a Kantian disjunction of mind and reality, and his concept of human nature only has explanatory power if the concept of nature means an unchanging substance that is independent of the mind. Chesterton would also agree with McCullagh's statement that historical knowledge and everyday knowledge are similar. Chesterton's emphasis on the common person and on common sense coincides with this belief that history is accessible to ordinary ways of thinking.

On the other hand, Hayden White's emphasis on literary forms as the key to the expression and interpretation of historical events bears some similarity to Chesterton's own attempt to present the coherence of history through stories and poetry. Chesterton, however, would not view history as an instrument to validate the historian's particular objectives, whether moral, aesthetic, or political, but instead as a real, but imperfect expression of some abiding truth about humanity's life in time.

In any event, separated as they are by temporal distance and a diversity of contexts, comparisons of Chesterton's views on history and the views of postmodern theorists are necessarily limited in value.

6 Conclusion
Locality, Patriotism, and Nationalism and One Lens More

As we have seen in the previous chapters, Chesterton expresses his philosophy of history in a variety of forms. This book has been primarily concerned with three of those forms; the private, psychological form of the novel, the oral and public form of the poetry, and the analytical, discursive form of his critical works. Based on the observations that have been made concerning these three approaches, I draw several conclusions about Chesterton's legacy in the area of the philosophy of history. Chesterton finds coherence in history to be a result of locality. A locality is where a person grows and exercises free will surrounded by a specific terrain, customs, language, and spiritual culture. Patriotism and nationalism are outgrowths of locality. The former tends to a love of one's own locality without a corresponding antagonism toward another, while the latter tends to dissatisfaction and consequent antagonism.

Chesterton gives prime importance to free will in all of his considerations regarding history. In *The Ballad of the White Horse*, Alfred's actions are contrasted with the despairing worldview of his enemies who are governed by a concept of fate that holds them in an iron grip. Alfred, on the other hand, remains cheerful even in the face of great adversity because his freedom is exercised in cooperation with a larger freedom that upholds his own good as well as the good of creation. ("The men of the East may spell the stars/ And times and triumphs mark/ But the men signed of the cross of Christ/ Go gaily in the dark."[1]) The simple fact of a Creator has extensive implications for Chesterton not only because it implies that all things are the result of a free choice leading to man's freedom being exercised within a larger freedom, but also because the world thereby becomes intelligible.

Chesterton revisits this theme in a different historical period in *Lepanto*. He compares the fatalism of Islam with the contingency and freedom of Christianity. By contrasting the arrogant presumption of the Turks with the cheerful abandon of Don John of Austria, Chesterton reiterates the paradoxical quality of human freedom as its exercise calls for decisiveness without a sure knowledge of success. The only way that success can be made possible is through an act of faith. Chesterton likens this quality of human freedom to a man making an appointment with himself sometime in the future without any sure knowledge that he will be able to keep it.

Chesterton's historical ballads highlight what he considers to be the pedagogical uses of history because of their oral and public form. The poetic form with its compressed meaning and rhythmic dimension is conducive to oral expression and therefore simultaneously accessible to a wide public. The English people were able to integrate both these kinds of poetic expression into their experience in a way that was not possible with the novel form. A striking confirmation of this effect was seen when, in the critical moments of World War II, the headlines of the British newspapers were emblazoned with quotes from *The Ballad of the White Horse*.[2]

Chesterton's own experience as a journalist and a polemicist gave him wide exposure to public oral forms of exposition, and convinced him of the importance of this instant, unmediated contact with the common man. It is not insignificant that Chesterton died in 1936 and his ballad was instrumental in stirring British morale in the long struggle of World War II. This is a striking example of his assertions about the democracy of the dead, whereby the truths and insights of one's predecessors continue to have a lasting effect. In this way, Chesterton participated in the reality of history and gave added weight to his contention that nothing is really lost to future generations when history is understood to be the living patrimony of every human being. This attitude is the reverse of ideological views of history, and looks at the past with an eye to preserving whatever is good in each historical epoch rather than taking a reactionary approach that simplifies complexity and eliminates the paradoxical. Chesterton gives vivid expression to this idea in his book *A Handful of Authors*:

> The modern world seems to have no notion of preserving different things side by side, of allowing its proper and proportionate place to each, of saving the whole varied heritage of culture.... I myself value the... nineteenth-century illumination of romantic love; just as I value the great eighteenth century ideal of right reason and human dignity, or the seventeenth century intensity, or the sixteenth century expansion, or the divine logic and dedicated valour of the Middle Ages.[3]

Although he is sometimes accused of being in debt to Belloc for his historical outlook, this passage would seem to indicate that Chesterton's vision of the past was capable of affirming and embracing a wider variety of viewpoints because of his attraction to whatever good could be found in them. It is hard to imagine Belloc affirming the exaltation of reason characteristic of eighteenth-century Europe, because it would mean looking past the excesses of thinkers such as Voltaire and Diderot and seeing the fundamental good that they pursued despite the excesses.

In one sense, Chesterton viewed the whole procession of the ages to be a progressive mosaic in which all the partial views of finite humanity were gradually assembled together into a single story. The limitations of each person, be they limitations of geography or climate, or just the common limitations imposed by a creaturely status, made it impossible for any one nation—let alone one individual—to be the chronicler of the story. To write any kind of meaningful history meant to make a bold selection from the vast ocean of human experience and attempt to convey the truth of it. In Chesterton's view, this could only be done without distortion by someone who was clear-sighted enough to look at reality with humility. In his view, this selection, however audacious, was not an exercise in futility precisely because of the connectedness in human affairs that was a direct result of the facts of creation and freedom. This made it not only possible to find coherence in history, but in a sense made it inevitable. Coherence and intelligibility are imbedded in reality through its origin. This is precisely why Chesterton was able to cite the deficiencies in the anti-essentialism of H.G. Wells's philosophy of history.

Chesterton's use of the private and psychological form of the novel stands in contrast to his use of the poetic form with its oral and public quality. The advantages he discerned in the novel came from the opportunity it provides for a detailed examination of states of mind and different philosophies. Chesterton's intuitive artistic mind prevented him from approaching different philosophies through the medium of an abstract syllogistic exposition, and naturally led him to take up a literary form.

Like Sir Walter Scott, Chesterton made use of vivid description and colorful details in an attempt to bring his characters to life. By encapsulating different approaches to reality in the vividly drawn characters of his novels, Chesterton was able to explore the interaction of these ideas in some detail and give the reader pictures of the ideas as if they were alive. This approach is similar to Scott's approach in a novel such as *Ivanhoe*, where he juxtaposes the Norman hegemony of Bois Gilbert with the Saxon patriotism of Athelred and the pragmatic synthesis of Wilfred of Ivanhoe. Scott found the novel to be the most effective tool for conveying the confluence of historical forces and ideas. Although Scott's artistry is considerably greater than Chesterton's, it is clear that Chesterton is attempting something similar, albeit with more emphasis on paradox and a heightened ambiguity that verges on science fiction. Here, the influence of Wells is apparent even though the philosophical points conveyed are divergent.

Chesterton uses his novels as a kind of colorful theatre in which he can watch different approaches to reality interact with each other, engaging in dialogue and monologue while the reader identifies with them and is brought to a clearer vision of the complexity of history. *The Ball and the Cross, The Napoleon of Notting Hill* and *The Man Who Was Thursday* demonstrate, each in its own way, the paradoxical structures that are at work in human history. MacIan and Turnbull represent an atheism and a theism in a battle that finds its resolution through uncovering the deeper reality that both are men with historical reasons for their respective positions. They are faced with the common enemy of humanity, Professor Lucifer, whose clear-sighted if malevolent intelligence understands that their willingness to die for strongly-held beliefs is indicative of a self-abnegation that bears too much of an imprint of the Creator. In elaborating this theme, Chesterton again shows his determination to get to the bottom of things using a playful paradoxical approach that consistently finds goodness in unexpected places.

Similarly, the experiences of Adam Wayne and Auberon Quin present a starkly drawn dichotomy that, by the novel's end, is deconstructed and reassembled to reveal both characters as the indispensable halves of an integral view of reality. Adam Wayne is the character who embodies local patriotism and goes to war to defend his neighborhood, but ironically in guaranteeing the autonomy of Notting Hill, he succeeds too well and is eventually attacked by the surrounding municipalities whose own sense of patriotism is aroused when Notting Hill becomes dominant. Here again, Chesterton succeeds in conveying the contingency of history that is a result of human freedom, specific locality and the continual fluid movement of the present slipping into the past. No one in the novel could have predicted the ironic outcome of the events that so thoroughly engrossed Wayne, Barker, Wilson and Quin. However, irony has the last word in the final conversation between the spirits of Quin and Wayne in that Wayne discovers humor and Quin becomes more serious. Each character is in need of the other because the patriot without humor fails to see the claims of other patriots, and the ruler who is completely unserious ignores the legitimate demands of human dignity.

The Man Who Was Thursday continues the exploration of the psychological aspect of history by exploring the rebel and the patriot that coexist inside each person. A dissatisfaction with the reality of a creation whose existence is anterior to human will offers each person the possibility of rebellion and anarchy. At the same time, as a direct result of being a creature, each person is free to affirm and protect the limited but valuable portion of creation entrusted to him; in other words, his locality. When Syme stands up before the council at the novel's end and declares his understanding of why he had to suffer, he is echoing Chesterton's oft-stated theme that it is only by suffering the loss of what we take for granted that we come to a renewed and deeper appreciation of it. The patriot in Chesterton's lexicon is the grateful participant in history who, like Wayne, fights doggedly to defend the beauty of his home, while the rebel is the nationalist who, like Lucian Gregory, finds the whole world too small to satisfy his ambition.

It is clear that Chesterton returns to the theme of locality again and again, using various forms, but always with the goal of presenting some new aspect of this multi-faceted reality for consideration. In his critical works, he looks at three different temperaments from three different historical periods, and examines their respective approaches to the theme of locality: Chaucer in the fourteenth-century, Cobbett in the late eighteenth to early nineteenth-century, and Dickens in the mid to late nineteenth-century.

In his specifically critical writings, Chesterton takes the stance of an evaluator of the creations of others, rather than that of a creator himself. This work of evaluation engages his artistic and analogical mind in a historical exercise of a different kind. Whereas in his novels and poems Chesterton is attempting to have others identify with his mind, in his critical work he undertakes the effort to identify his mind with others. It is an exercise in historical imagination. In his essay entitled "Where Chesterton Comes In", McLuhan isolates this ability as one of Chesterton's salient qualities:

> ... he had no difficulty in imagining what sort of psychological pressures would occur in the mind of a fourth-century Egyptian, or a Highland clansman, or a modern Californian, popping himself inside of them and seeing with their eyes ... [4]

In examining Geoffrey Chaucer and his work, Chesterton makes good use of this imaginative power to arrive at a balanced understanding of Chaucer's place in English history while avoiding the danger of changing Chaucer into a man of his own time. Instead, Chesterton saw a competent official of the court whose keen eye and vivid imagination transmuted the tumultuous material of his century into something permanent. In so doing, he put the fledgling English language on a firm footing and combined the disparate threads of Christian, classical, French and German influences into a texture that would serve as the woof upon which the English nation would be woven.

Chesterton gives particular credit to Chaucer's optimism, which allowed him to sympathize with his characters in much the same way Charles Dickens did. While not ignoring the genuine evil in his world—a trait clearly evident in his depiction of the Pardoner—Chaucer nonetheless saw the essential goodness underlying the varying choices of individuals. This vision along with his talent enabled him to remain loyal to his nascent culture and make an enormous contribution to its growth. For this reason, Chesterton sees him as a father figure and a patriot who embraced his locality, participated in its life, and left an enduring stamp upon it.

In a figure such as William Cobbett, Chesterton detects a patriotism similar to that of Chaucer in its intensity, but expressed through a more melancholic temperament and a less powerful poetic talent. Cobbett's literary product took the form of journalistic expression and the chronicling of a vanishing rural way of life. Unlike Chaucer, Cobbett's criticism of the governing structures of his society took a more direct form and is probably less enduring for his not having been capable of transforming his reactions into a work of art. Nonetheless, Chesterton sees in him a strong expression of the attachment to the local terrain and climate that is an essential component of his conception of patriotism.

Cobbett lived in an age when the doctrines of the physiocrats were finding influential expression in both the old and new worlds. But unlike a man such as Thomas Jefferson, Cobbett was too deeply rooted in the historic religion of his ancestors to place his hopes in nature alone. This peculiar combination of adherence to an ancient faith and a loving attachment to the local characteristics of his country made Cobbett resonate strongly with Chesterton because the combination was so rarely to be found in an Englishman of Cobbett's era. In one sense, Chesterton sees Cobbett as continuing the patriotic tradition of Chaucer, but with an added dimension. By virtue of his place in history, Cobbett witnessed the beginnings of the Industrial Revolution, capitalism in England, and the resulting changes that would permanently affect the human and political landscape of his country. Chesterton saw Cobbett as a prophet who warned of the loss of the average Englishman's power of self-support through the centralization of capital and resources. Like the present-day political philosopher Chantal Millon-Delsol, Cobbett advocated the exercise of political and economic authority at the most local level possible in order to be effective. In his championing of the small landholder and the local exercise of authority, Cobbett was an early proponent of the idea that mediating institutions allowed for a more humane exercise of power.

In a similar vein, Charles Dickens lived to see the full flowering of these tendencies that Cobbett had discerned in their early growth. The nineteenth century in which Dickens lived had become the century when the common man, more than ever before in English history, could reach the point of wielding authority and power over his fellow men. For the first time, the middle class was a potent reality. The forces that Cobbett had warned of were now in full play. But if the middle class was shown to be capable of just as much evil as their former aristocratic masters, they were also capable of great good.

Dickens became the chronicler of the moral life of the common Englishman, something that Chaucer had barely touched on because of the limitations of his age. The novel was the adequate instrument for a detailed exploration of the almost endless psychological possibilities offered by the newly empowered class. Chesterton named Dickens the last of the great men precisely because Dickens was capable of looking at this newly constructed stage of the urban industrial world and finding heroic figures that compared favorably with Chaucer's knights and clerics.

Even though the conditions of his country had changed dramatically within the course of a hundred years, Dickens was the true patriot in Chesterton's understanding of that term because he was not ready to abandon his locality, but instead decided to paint its literary portrait over and over again with a truthful eye. Judging from the overflowing crowds who came to hear him read his novels, Dickens' portraits were well-received by the common people who were delighted to see themselves imitated in both their good and bad aspects.

Dickens's eager participation in the public life of his fellow men makes him a kindred spirit to Chesterton as well as to Chaucer. Although he used the more private form of the novel, his theatrical background made it possible for him to transmit it in a very public, oral way. What separates Chaucer and Dickens from Cobbett is that most pervasive Chestertonian quality of humor. Cobbett saw the serious side of things, but Chaucer and Dickens could see more deeply because they perceived the humorous side as well.

This one important quality is a key that unifies Chesterton's historical philosophy. Because humor involves seeing one thing under multiple aspects, the writer who has a sense of humor will by definition be able to sense the multiple meanings inherent in any aspect of reality. Also, because any given historical event could have been played out differently, Chesterton was keenly aware that an over-serious approach to life would stand in the way of a full acknowledgment of human freedom. In *The Ball and the Cross*, for example, although MacIan is a Christian and therefore, one would suppose, more sympathetic in Chesterton's eyes, he lacks the essential sense of humor and thus cannot conceive that things could be seen in any way other than his own. It never occurs to him that his enemy, Turnbull, although an atheist, is also a free man like himself and thus capable of taking many turns in his path before he comes to the end of it. In addition, there is the example of Adam Wayne in *The Napoleon of Nottting Hill*, whose deadly serious espousal of local patriotism might seem to be the very embodiment of Chesterton's view. But Chesterton has his character slain and afterwards enlightened by Auberon Quin, whose sense of humor provides the vital corrective to Wayne's partial view of reality.

The sense of irony and a sense of humor are two ways of naming the notion that things are not to be read in only one way. In a world that is pre-determined, a sense of humor would be superfluous. But in a world that is the result of an overarching divine freedom and a multiplicity of human freedoms, a sense of play must be added to a sense of seriousness if the reality of history is to be truly presented. In an article entitled, "If Don John of Austria Had Married Mary Queen of Scots," Chesterton playfully takes up a historical possibility that never came to be.

> There is perhaps, therefore, something more than a fancy, certainly something more than an accident, in this connection between the two romantic figures and the great turning point of history. They might really have turned it to the right rather than the left; or at least prevented it from turning too far to the left.[5]

This imaginative exercise stands as a type of model for his approach to history that places greater emphasis on literary forms than expository prose. The literary forms, whether poetry or prose, use the imagination as the only instrument capable of the compression and expansion of events, so that the most enduring and significant elements of history can be properly underscored. And perhaps just as importantly, these forms allow for the wide dispersal and eager reception of historical truth. Without such a transmittal and reception, history remains the province of a few and loses it power to influence the present and the future.

Notes

NOTES TO THE INTRODUCTION

1. John Sullivan, editor, *G.K Chesterton: A Centenary Appraisal* (New York: Harper& Row Publishers, Inc. 1974), 3-15.
2. Gilbert K. Chesterton, *A Short History of England* (New York: John Lane Company, 1917), 108.
3. For a thorough exploration of the growth of state-centered historical analysis see Christopher Dawson, *Progress and Religion* (London: 1929). Chesterton's influence on Dawson's historical thought is examined in chapter 5.
4. Raymond Las Vergnas, *Chesterton, Belloc, Baring*, trans. C.C. Martindale, S.J. (New York: Sheed & Ward, 1938), 48.
5. G. K. Chesterton, *Heretics* (London: The Bodley Head Ltd., 1905), 253.
6. G. K. Chesterton, *As I Was Saying* (New York: Dodd, Mead & Company, 1936), 118
7. G.K. Chesterton, *The Common Man* (New York: Sheed and Ward, 1950), 50, 52.
8. See, for example, G.K. Chesterton, *St. Thomas Aquinas* (New York: Sheed and Ward, 1954), 220-225.
9. Ian Boyd, *The Novels of G.K. Chesterton: A Study in Art and Propaganda* (New York: Harper & Row Publishers, Inc., 1975), 11.

NOTES TO CHAPTER 1

1. Eric Hobsbawm, *On History* (New York: The New Press, 1997), 59.
2. G. K. Chesterton, *The Everlasting Man* (San Francisco: Ignatius Press, 1993), [copyright 1925 Dodd, Mead & Company, Inc]., 139–141.
3. Eric Hobsbawm, *On History* (New York: The New Press, 1997), 9.
4. Sylvere Monod, "The Uses and Varieties of Imagination in G.K. Chesterton's *The Everlasting Man*," *The Chesterton Review* 13.1 (1987):55.
5. Ibid., 69.
6. Ernest Gellner, *Nations and Nationalism* (Ithaca: Cornell University Press, 1983), 43.
7. Ibid., 1.
8. Ibid., 48.
9. G. K. Chesterton, *The New Jerusalem* (New York: George H. Doran Company, 1921), 40.
10. G. K. Chesterton, *The Appetite of Tyranny* (New York: Dodd, Mead & Co., 1915), 44.

11. G.K. Chesterton, *The Autobiography of G.K.Chesterton* (New York: Sheed & Ward, 1936), 128.
12. Michael Coren, *Gilbert: The Man Who Was G.K. Chesterton* (New York: Paragon House, 1990), 223.
13. Ibid., 245, 248.
14. Hugh Kenner, *Paradox in Chesterton* (New York: Sheed & Ward, 1947), 15.
15. Ibid., 17.
16. Ibid., 67–68.
17. G.K. Chesterton, *St. Thomas Aquinas* (New York: Sheed and Ward, 1954), 104–109.
18. Ibid., 139–140.
19. Quentin Lauer, S.J., *G.K. Chesterton: Philosopher Without Portfolio* (New York: Fordham University Press, 1988), 19.
20. Ibid., 62–63.
21. Ibid., 161.
22. G. K. Chesterton, *The Everlasting Man* (San Francisco: Ignatius Press, 1993), 263.
23. William T. Scott, *Chesterton and Other Essays* (Cincinnati: Jennings and Graham, 1912), 17.
24. Ibid., 12.
25. Ibid., 44.
26. Ibid., 19.
27. W.R. Titterton, *G.K. Chesterton: A Portrait* (Folcroft, Pa.: Folcroft Library Editions, 1974), 53.
28. Ibid., 85.
29. G. K. Chesterton, *The Ballad of the White Horse* (Edited by Bernadette Sheridan, IHM, Detroit: Marygrove College Press, 1993), 73.
30. Michael Ffinch, *G.K. Chesterton: A Biography* (San Francisco: Harper & Row Publishers, 1986), 181.
31. G. K. Chesterton, *What's Wrong With The World* (San Francisco: Ignatius Press, 1910), 84.
32. Michael Ffinch, *G.K. Chesterton: A Biography* (San Francisco: Harper & Row Publishers, 1986), 276–277.
33. G. K. Chesterton, *Alarms and Discursions* (New York: Dodd, Mead & Company, 1911), 148.
34. Ian Boyd, *The Novels of G.K. Chesterton: A Study in Art and Propaganda* (New York: Harper & Row Publishers, Inc., 1975), 198.
35. Ibid., 198.
36. John Sullivan, editor, *G.K. Chesterton: A Centenary Appraisal* (New York: Harper & Row Publishers, Inc. 1974), 47–48.
37. Ibid., 3, 11.
38. Ibid., 14.
39. Dudley Barker, *G.K. Chesterton* (New York: Stein and Day, 1973), 141.
40. Ibid., 176.
41. Jay P. Corrin, *G.K. Chesterton & Hilaire Belloc: The Battle Against Modernity* (Athens/London: Ohio University Press, 1981), 136.
42. Ibid., 136–137.
43. Christopher Hollis, *The Mind of Chesterton* (Coral Gables: University of Miami Press, 1970), 166.
44. Maisie Ward, *Return to Chesterton* (New York: Sheed and Ward, 1952), 54–55.
45. Joseph Pearce, *Wisdom and Innocence* (San Francisco: Ignatius Press, 1996), 378–379.

46. Alzina Stone Dale, *The Outline of Sanity: A Biography of G.K. Chesterton* (Grand Rapids: William B. Eerdmans Publishing Company, 1982), 161–162.
47. Ibid., 162.
48. Garry Wills, *Chesterton: Man and Mask* (New York: Sheed & Ward, 1961), 99.
49. Ibid., 99, 101.
50. Ibid., 104–105.
51. Ibid., 152.
52. Chantal Millon-Delsol: *L'État Subsidiare: Ingérence et non-ingérence de l'Etat: le principe de subsidiarité aux fondements de l'histoire européene* (Paris: Presses universitaires de France, 1992), 5.
53. Ibid., 5–6.
54. Ibid., 7.
55. Ibid., 97.
56. Ibid., 163.
57. Ibid., 164–165.

NOTES TO CHAPTER 2

1. Hazard Adams & Leroy Searle, eds., *Critical Theory Since 1965* (Tallahassee: Florida State University Press, 1986), 332.
2. Ibid., 331.
3. D.J. Conlon, Editor, *G.K. Chesterton: A Half Century of Views* (Oxford: Oxford University Press, 1987), 39.
4. G.K. Chesterton, *The Autobiography of G.K.Chesterton* (New York: Sheed & Ward, 1936), 301–302.
5. Gilbert K. Chesterton, *A Miscellany of Men* (New York: Dodd, Mead & Company, 1912), 172.
6. Raymond Las Vergnas, *Chesterton, Belloc, Baring* (New York: Sheed & Ward, 1938 translated by C.C. Martindale, S.J.), 65.
7. Ibid., v, vi.
8. G. K. Chesterton, *The Everlasting Man* (San Francisco: Ignatius Press, 1993), 61.
9. G.K. Chesterton, *Heretics* (London: The Bodley Head Ltd., 1960), 74.
10. Ibid., 74–75.
11. G. K. Chesterton, *The Everlasting Man* (San Francisco: Ignatius Press, 1993), 75.
12. Ibid., 104.
13. Ibid., 157.
14. Gilbert K. Chesterton, *George Bernard Shaw* (New York: John Land Company, 1909), 68–69.
15. Ibid., 176.
16. Ibid., 175.
17. Gilbert K. Chesterton, *A Miscellany of Men* (New York: Dodd, Mead & Company, 1912), 186.
18. Ibid., 238.
19. Henry Thomas Buckle, *History of Civilization in England* (London: J.W. Parker, 1857), 209.
20. Ibid., 205.
21. William Edward Hartpole Lecky, *Historical and Political Essays* (New York: Longmans, Green, and Co., 1908), 4.
22. Ibid., 20.

23. G. P. Gooch, *History and Historians in the Nineteenth Century* (Boston: Beacon Press, 1959), 333.
24. John Richard Green, *A Short History of the English People* (London: Macmillan and Co., 1881), 155.
25. Ibid., 189.
26. G. P. Gooch, *History and Historians in the Nineteenth Century* (Boston: Beacon Press, 1959), 315.
27. James Anthony Froude, *Short Studies on Great Subjects* (New York: Charles Scribner's Sons, 1864), 35.
28. Ibid., 34.
29. J.E.E.D. Acton, *Essays in the Liberal Interpretation of History* (Chicago: University of Chicago Press, 1967), 302.
30. Ibid., 312.
31. Ibid., 419.
32. G.K. Chesterton, *Generally Speaking* (New York: Dodd, Mead & Co., 1929), 182.
33. Ibid., 180.
34. Gerald Bullett, *The Innocence of G.K. Chesteron* (New York: Henry Holt and Company, 1925), 91.
35. Maisie Ward, *Return to Chesterton* (New York: Sheed and Ward, 1952), 290.
36. G. K. Chesterton, *The Autobiography of G. K. Chesterton* (New York: Sheed and Ward, 1936), 144–145.
37. G. K Chesterton, *William Cobbett* (New York: Dodd, Mead & Company, 1926), 63.
38. Ibid., 249.
39. Ibid., 133.
40. G. K. Chesterton, *Varied Types* (New York: Books for Libraries Press, Inc., 1903), 163.
41. Ibid., 167–168.
42. G. K. Chesterton, *All I Survey: A Book of Essays* (New York: Dodd, Mead & Company, 1933), 264.
43. Ibid., 266.

NOTES TO CHAPTER 3

1. G. K. Chesterton, *Lunacy & Letters* (London and New York: Sheed and Ward, 1958), 130.
2. Noel O'Donoghue, "Chesterton and the Philosophical Imagination," *The Chesterton Review* 24.1–2 (1998), 68.
3. G. K. Chesterton, *Lunacy & Letters* (London and New York: Sheed and Ward, 1958), 131–132.
4. G. K. Chesterton, *Chaucer* (New York: Sheed and Ward, 1956), 5.
5. G. K. Chesterton, *All I Survey: A Book of Essays* (New York: Dodd, Mead & Company, 1933), 213–214.
6. G. K. Chesterton, *Chaucer* (New York: Sheed and Ward, 1956), 245.
7. G. K. Chesterton, *All I Survey: A Book of Essays* (New York: Dodd, Mead & Company, 1933), 209.
8. Gilbert K. Chesterton, *A Short History of England* (New York: John Lane Company, 1917), 67.
9. Josef Pieper, *In Tune With the World: A Theory of Festivity* (Chicago: Franciscan Herald Press, 1973), 11.

10. Gilbert K. Chesterton, *A Short History of England* (New York: John Lane Company, 1917), 106–107.
11. G. K. Chesterton, *Eugenics & Other Evils* (New York: Dodd, Mead & Company, 1927), 115.
12. G. K. Chesterton, *Lunacy & Letters* (London and New York: Sheed and Ward, 1958), 132.
13. G. K. Chesterton, *What's Wrong with the World* (eighth edition, London: Cassell and Company, Limited, 1910), 101.
14. Patrick Braybrooke, *Gilbert Keith Chesterton* (London: The Chelsea Publishing Company, 1973), 58.
15. Johan Huizinga, *The Waning of the Middle Ages: A Study of the Forms of Life, Thought, and Art in France and the Netherlands in the XIVth and XVth Centuries* (New York: St. Martin's Press, 1969).
16. G.K. Chesterton, *Saint Thomas Aquinas* (San Francisco: St. Ignatius Press, 2002), 9.
17. G. K. Chesterton, *Chaucer* (New York: Sheed and Ward, 1956), 121.
18. G. K. Chesterton, *The Superstition of Divorce* (London: Chatto & Windus, 1920), 116.
19. G. K. Chesterton, *Chaucer* (New York: Sheed and Ward, 1956), 184.
20. G. K. Chesterton, *Lunacy & Letters* (London and New York: Sheed and Ward, 1958), 54.
21. G. K. Chesterton, *The Victorian Age in Literature* (London: Oxford University Press, 1913), 153.
22. Ibid., 49.
23. Patrick Braybrooke, *Gilbert Keith Chesterton* (London: The Chelsea Publishing Company, 1973), 10.
24. G.K. Chesterton, *The Autobiography of G.K.Chesterton* (New York: Sheed & Ward, 1936), 204–205.
25. G. K. Chesterton, *The Victorian Age in Literature* (London: Oxford University Press, 1913), 14.
26. Ibid., 25.
27. Ibid., 147.
28. G. K. Chesterton, *What I Saw in America* (New York: Dodd, Mead & Company, 1922), 114.
29. G. K. Chesterton, *A Handful of Authors: Essays on Books and Writers* (New York: Sheed and Ward, 1953), 175.
30. G. K. Chesterton, *The Victorian Age in Literature* (London: Oxford University Press, 1913), 8.
31. Dorothy Collins, Editor, *G.K. Chesterton, A Handful of Authors: Essays on Books & Writers* (New York: Sheed and Ward, 1953), 55.
32. G. K. Chesterton, *A Handful of Authors: Essays on Books and Writers* (New York: Sheed and Ward, 1953), 168–169.
33. G.K. Chesterton, *The Autobiography of G.K.Chesterton* (New York: Sheed & Ward, 1936), 13.
34. G. K. Chesterton, *Appreciations and Criticisms of the Works of Charles Dickens* (New York: Haskell House Publishers Ltd., 1970), 135.
35. G.K. Chesterton, *The Autobiography of G.K.Chesterton* (New York: Sheed & Ward, 1936), 90–91.
36. G.K. Chesterton, *Charles Dickens, The Last of the Great Men* (New York: The Press of the Readers Club, 1906), 12.
37. Ibid., 8.
38. Ibid., 179–180.
39. G. K. Chesterton, *Appreciations and Criticisms of the Works of Charles Dickens* (New York: Haskell House Publishers Ltd., 1970), 167.

40. John Coates, *Chesterton and the Edwardian Cultural Crisis* (Pickering: Hull University Press, 1984), 98.
41. Dorothy Collins, Editor, *G.K. Chesterton, A Handful of Authors: Essays on Books & Writers* (New York: Sheed and Ward, 1953), 45.
42. G.K. Chesterton, *Charles Dickens, The Last of the Great Men* (New York: The Press of the Readers Club, 1942), 22.
43. G. K. Chesterton, *The Uses of Diversity* (New York: Dodd, Mead and Company, 1921), 118.

NOTES TO CHAPTER 4

1. G. K. Chesterton, *The Napoleon of Notting Hill* (Beaconsfield: Darwen Finlayson Limited, 1964), 9.
2. G. K. Chesterton, *The Everlasting Man* (San Francisco: Ignatius Press, 1993), [copyright 1925 Dodd, Mead & Company, Inc.], 140.
3. G. K. Chesterton, *The Ball and the Cross* (Beaconsfield: Darwen Finlayson Limited, 1963), 70.
4. Ibid., 132.
5. Ibid., 132.
6. Ibid., 133.
7. Ibid., 34.
8. Ibid., 26.
9. Ibid., 27.
10. Ibid., 202.
11. Ibid., 191.
12. Gilbert K. Chesterton, *A Short History of England* (New York: John Lane Company, 1917), 49.
13. G. K. Chesterton, *The Ball and the Cross* (Beaconsfield: Darwen Finlayson Limited, 1963), 238.
14. Ibid., 240.
15. G. K. Chesterton, *The Napoleon of Notting Hill* (Beaconsfield: Darwen Finlayson Limited, 1964), 47.
16. Ibid., 50.
17. Ibid., 78.
18. Ibid., 27.
19. Ibid., 45.
20. Ibid., 32.
21. Ibid., 86.
22. Ibid., 87.
23. Ibid., 192.
24. Lawrence John Zillman, *The Art and Craft of Poetry* (New York: Collier Books, 1967), 129–134.
25. G. K. Chesterton, *The Ballad of the White Horse*, (Sisters, Servants of the Immaculate Heart of Mary, Monroe, Michigan. Edited by Bernadette Sheridan, IHM, Detroit: Marygrove College Press, 1993), 11.
26. Ibid., 16–17.
27. Ibid., 22.
28. Ibid., 22–23.
29. Ibid., 30–31.
30. Ibid., 36.
31. Ibid., 58.
32. Ibid., 62.
33. Ibid., 80.

34. Ibid., 82.
35. Ibid., 101.
36. Ibid., 129.
37. Ibid., 146.
38. G.K. Chesterton, *The Collected Poems of G.K. Chesterton* (London: Methuen & Company, 1933), 117.
39. Ibid., 115.
40. Ibid., 115.
41. Ibid., 117- 121.
42. Ibid., 118.
43. G. K. Chesterton, *Selected Essays of G. K. Chesterton* (London: Methuen and Company, Ltd., 1949), 206.
44. Ibid., 207–208.
45. Joseph Pearce, *Wisdom and Innocence: A Life of G. K. Chesterton* (San Francisco: Ignatius Press, 1996), 183.
46. G.K. Chesterton, *The Collected Poems of G.K. Chesterton* (London: Methuen & Company, 1933), 117.
47. Ibid., 121.
48. G.K. Chesterton, *The Man Who Was Thursday: A Nightmare* (New York: Sheed and Ward, 1975), 10.
49. Ibid., 11.
50. Gilbert K. Chesterton, *Orthodoxy* (Westport: Greenwood Press, 1974), 73.
51. G.K. Chesterton, *The Man Who Was Thursday: A Nightmare* (New York: Sheed and Ward, 1975), 12.
52. Ibid., 42.
53. Ibid., 190.
54. Ibid., 49.
55. Ibid., 197.

NOTES TO CHAPTER 5

1. Christina Scott, *A Historian and His World: A Life of Christopher Dawson 1889–1970* (London: Sheed & Ward, 1984), 71.
2. Ibid., 74.
3. Christopher Dawson, *The Making of Europe: An Introduction to the History Of European Unity* (New York: The World Publishing Company, 1966), 20–21.
4. G. K. Chesterton, *The New Jerusalem* (New York: George H. Doran Company, 1921), 33.
5. Christina Scott, *A Historian and His World: A Life of Christopher Dawson 1889–1970* (London: Sheed & Ward, 1984), 103.
6. G. K. Chesterton, *The Ballad of the White Horse* (Edited by Bernadette Sheridan, IHM, Detroit: Marygrove College Press, 1993), xxxvi.
7. Classics scholar Susanna Braund of Yale University comments on Virgil's similar accomplishment in *The Aeneid*: "What is different about Virgil's achievement in *The Aeneid* is the way in which he builds material of historical, political and religious significance to his contemporaries into a narrative of the events of just one year set in the distant past." Susanna Morton Braund, *Latin Literature* (London: Routledge Publishing Co., 2002) 7.
8. Christina Scott, *A Historian and His World: A Life of Christopher Dawson 1889–1970* (London: Sheed & Ward, 1984), 104–105.
9. Christopher Dawson, *Religion and the Rise of Western Culture* (New York: Sheed & Ward, 1950), 211.

10. G. K. Chesterton, *The Ballad of the White Horse* (Edited by Bernadette Sheridan, IHM, Detroit: Marygrove College Press, 1993), 61.
11. Christopher Dawson, *The Making of Europe: An Introduction to the History Of European Unity* (New York: The World Publishing Company, 1966), 19.
12. Gilbert K. Chesterton, *A Short History of England* (New York: John Lane Company, 1917), 53.
13. Martin Stannard, *Evelyn Waugh: The Early Years 1903–1939* (London: J. M. Dent and Sons, Ltd., 1986), 456.
14. Donat Gallagher, Editor, *The Essays, Articles and Reviews of Evelyn Waugh* (Boston: Little, Brown and Company, 1984), 334–335.
15. In a 1961 review of Gary Wills' *Chesterton: Man and Mask*, Waugh was effusive in his praise of Chesterton's book and its influence. Referring to Wills, Waugh says, "For him, as for this reviewer, Chesterton is primarily the author of *The Everlasting Man*. In that book all his random thoughts are concentrated and refined; all his aberrations made straight. It is a great, popular book, one of the few really great popular books of the century; the triumphant assertion that a book can be both great and popular needs no elucidation. It is brilliantly clear. It met a temporary need and survives as a permanent monument." Ibid., 560.
16. Martin Stannard, *Evelyn Waugh: The Early Years 1903–1939* (London: J. M. Dent and Sons, Ltd., 1986), 389.
17. Evelyn Waugh, *Edmund Campion* (New York: Sheed & Ward Inc., 1935), 37–38.
18. Ibid., 172.
19. Martin Stannard, *Evelyn Waugh: The Early Years 1903–1939* (London: J. M. Dent and Sons, Ltd., 1986), 392.
20. Evelyn Waugh, *Brideshead Revisited* (Boston: Little, Brown and Company, 1945), 351.
21. D.J. Conlon, Editor, *G.K. Chesterton: A Half Century of Views* (Oxford: Oxford University Press, 1987), 74.
22. Ibid., 74.
23. Ibid., 2.
24. W. Terrence Gordon, *Marshall McLuhan: Escape into Understanding, A Biography* (New York: Harper Collins Publishing Inc., 1997), 32.
25. Ibid., 11–12.
26. Ibid., 54.
27. Ibid., 38, 54.
28. Ibid., 48.
29. D.J. Conlon, Editor, *G.K. Chesterton: A Half Century of Views* (Oxford: Oxford University Press, 1987), 7.
30. W. Terrence Gordon, *Marshall McLuhan: Escape into Understanding, A Biography* (New York: Harper Collins Publishing Inc., 1997), 104–105.
31. D.J. Conlon, Editor, *G.K. Chesterton: A Half Century of Views* (Oxford: Oxford University Press, 1987), 75–76.
32. Ibid., 6.
33. Hayden White, *Metahistory* (Baltimore: Johns Hopkins UP, 1973) 21.
34. Ibid., 9.
35. Hayden White, *Tropics of Discourse* (Baltimore: Johns Hopkins UP, 1978),56.
36. Ibid., 54.
37. C.Behan McCullagh, : "The Truth of Historical Narratives," *History and Theory* 26.4 (1987):31.
38. Ibid.,33.

39. Ibid., 33.
40. See, for example, Thomas L. Haskell, "Objectivity in Not Neutrality, Rhetoric vs. Practice in Peter Novick's That Noble Dream," *History and Theory* 29 (1990): 129–157. Peter Novick, *That Noble Dream: The "Objectivity Question" and the American Historical Profession* (Cambridge University Press, 1988);

NOTES TO CHAPTER 6

1. G. K. Chesterton, *The Ballad of the White Horse* (Edited by Bernadette Sheridan, IHM, Detroit: Marygrove College Press, 1993), 15.
2. Ibid.,211.
3. G.K. Chesterton, *A Handful of Authors* (New York: Sheed & Ward, 1953), 195–196.
4. D.J. Conlon, Editor, *G.K. Chesterton: A Half Century of Views* (Oxford: Oxford University Press, 1987), 77.
5. G.K. Chesterton, *The Common Man* (New York: Sheed & Ward, 1950), 276.

Bibliography

PRIMARY SOURCES

Chesterton, G.K. *Varied Types*. New York: Books for Libraries Press, Inc., 1903.
———. *The Napoleon of Notting Hill*. New York and London: J. Lane, 1904.
———. *Heretics*. London: The Bodley Head Ltd., 1905.
———. *The Man Who Was Thursday: A Nightmare*. New York: Dodd, Mead & Company, 1908.
———. *The Ball and the Cross*. New York: J. Lane, 1909.
———. *George Bernard Shaw*. New York: John Land Company, 1909.
———. *What's Wrong With The World*. San Francisco: Ignatius Press, 1910.
———. *The Innocence of Fr. Brown*. London, New York: Cassell and Company, 1911.
———. *The Ballad of the White Horse*. London: Methuen and Company, Ltd, 1911
———. *Alarms and Discursions*. New York: Dodd, Mead & Co., 1911.
———. *A Miscellany of Men*. New York: Dodd, Mead & Co., 1912.
———. *Manalive*. New York, John Lane, 1912.
———. *Magic: A Fantastic Comedy*. London: M. Secker, 1913.
———. *The Victorian Age In Literature*. London: Oxford University Press, 1913.
———. *The Flying Inn*. New York: John Lane, 1914.
———. *The Wisdom of Fr. Brown*. London, New York: Cassell and Company, 1914.
———. *Poems*. New York: John Lane, 1915.
———. *The Appetite of Tyranny*. New York: Dodd, Mead & Co., 1915
———. *A Short History of England*. New York, John Lane Co., 1917.
———. *The Superstition of Divorce*. London: Chatto & Windus, 1920.
———. *The Uses of Diversity*. New York: Dodd, Mead and Company, 1921.
———. *The New Jerusalem*. New York: George H. Doran Co., 1921
———. *The Man Who Knew Too Much*. New York and London: Harper and Brothers, 1922.
———. *What I Saw in America*. New York: Dodd, Mead & Company, 1922.
———. *Saint Thomas* Aquinas San Francisco: St. Ignatius Press, 1986 (originally 1923).
———. *Tales of the Long Bow*. New York: Sheed and Ward, 1925.
———. *The Everlasting Man*. New York: Dodd, Mead & Co., 1925.
———. *William Cobbett*. New York: Dodd, Mead & Co., 1926.
———. *Eugenics & Other Evils*. New York: Dodd, Mead & Company, 1927.
———. *The Judgment of Dr. Johnson*. New York: London: G.P. Putnam's Sons, 1928.

152 Bibliography

―――. *Generally Speaking.* New York: Dodd, Mead & Co., 1929.
―――. *The Poet and the Lunatics.* New York: Dodd, Mead and Company, 1929.
―――. *Four Faultless Felons.* New York: Dodd, Mead and Company, 1930.
―――. *All I Survey.* New York: Dodd, Mead & Company, 1933.
―――. *The Collected Poems of G.K. Chesterton.* London: Methuen & Company, 1933.
―――. *The Scandal of Fr. Brown.* New York: Dodd, Mead and Company, 1935.
―――. *As I Was Saying.* New York: Dodd, Mead & Co., 1936.
―――. *The Autobiography of G.K. Chesteron.* New York, 1936.
―――. *The Paradoxes of Mr. Pond.* New York: Dodd, Mead and Company, 1937.
―――. *Charles Dickens. The Last of the Great Men,* New York: The Press of the Readers Club, 1942.
―――. *Selected Essays of G.K. Chesterton.* London: Methuen and Company, Ltd., 1949.
―――. *The Common Man.* New York: Sheed and Ward, 1950.
―――. *The Surprise.* New York, Sheed and Ward: 1952.
―――. *A Handful of Authors: Essays on Books and Writers.* New York: Sheed and Ward, 1953.
―――. *Chaucer.* New York: Sheed and Ward, 1956.
―――. *Lunacy & Letters.* London and New York: Sheed and Ward, 1958.
―――. *Appreciations and Criticisms of the Works of Charles Dickens.* New York: Haskell House Publishers Ltd, 1970.
―――. *Orthodoxy.* Westport: Greenwood Press, 1974.

SECONDARY SOURCES: BOOKS

Acton, J.E.E.D. *Essays In the Liberal Interpretation of History,* Chicago: University of Chicago Press, 1967.
Adams, Hazard and Searle, Leroy, eds. *Critical Theory Since 1965,* Tallahassee: Florida State University Press, 1986.
Attwater, Donald. *Modern Christian Revolutionaries: An Introduction to the Lives and Thought of Kierkegaard, Eric Gill, G.K. Chesterton, C.F. Andrews and Berdyaev.* Freeport, New York: Books For Libraries Press, 1971.
Auden, W.H. *G.K. Chesterton: A Selection from His Non-Fictional Prose.* London: Faber & Faber, 1970.
Barker, Dudley. *G. K. Chesterton.* New York: Stein and Day, 1973.
Baring, Maurice. *The Puppet Show of Memory.* Boston: Little, Brown, 1923.
Belloc, Hilaire. *On the Place of Gilbert Chesterton in English Letters.* New York: Sheed and Ward, 1940.
―――. *The Servile State.* Originally pub. 1913; rpt. Indianapolis: Liberty Press, 1979.
Bloom, Harold. *The Anxiety of Influence.* New York: Oxford University Press, 1973.
Boyd, Ian. *The Novels of G.K. Chesterton: A Study in Art and Propaganda.* London: Paul Elek, 1975.
Braund, Susanna Morton. *Latin Literature,* London: Routledge Publishing Co., 2002.
Braybrooke, Patrick. *Gilbert Keith Chesterton,* London: The Chelsea Publishing Company, 1973.
Buckle, Henry Thomas. *History of Civilization in England,* London: J.W. Parker, 1857.

Bullett, Gerald William. *The Innocence of G.K. Chesterton.* London: C. Palmer, 1925.
Canovan, Margaret. *G.K. Chesterton: Radical Populist.* New York: Harcourt Brace Jovanovich, 1977.
Chesterton, Ada (Mrs. Cecil). *The Chestertons.* London: Chapman & Hall, 1941.
Chesterton, Cecil. *G.K. Chesterton: A Criticism.* London: Alston Rivers, 1908.
Clipper, Lawrence. *G.K. Chesterton.* New York: Twayne Publishers, 1974.
Coates, John. *Chesterton and The Edwardian Cultural Crisis.* Hull, England: Hull University Library, 1984.
Collins, Dorothy, Editor. *G.K. Chesterton, A Handful of Authors: Essays on Books & Writers* New York: Sheed & Ward, 1953.
Conlon, D.J. ed. *G.K. Chesterton, A Half-Century of Views.* Oxford: Oxford University Press,1987.
Coren, Michael. *Gilbert: The Man Who Was G.K. Chesterton.* New York:Paragon House, 1990.
Corrin, Jay. *G.K. Chesterton and Hilaire Belloc: The Battle Against Modernity.* Athens, Ohio: Ohio University Press, 1981.
Crowther, Ian. *Chesterton.* London: Claridge Press, 1993.
Dale, Alzina Stone. *The Outline of Sanity: A Biography of G.K. Chesterton.* Grand Rapids: William B. Eerdmans, 1982.
Dawson, Christopher. *The Making of Europe: An Introduction to the History of European Unity.* Originally pub. 1932, rpt. New York: The World Publishing Co., 1966.
———. *Religion and the Rise of Western Culture*, New York: Sheed & Ward, 1950.
Ffinch, Michael. *G.K. Chesterton.* San Francisco: Harper and Row, 1986.
Froude, James Anthony. *Short Studies on Great Subjects,* New York: Charles Scribner's Sons, 1864.
Furlong, William B. *Shaw and Chesterton: The Metaphysical Jesters.* University Park: Pennsylvania State University Press, 1970.
Gallagher, Donat, *The essays, Articles and Reviews of Evelyn Waugh*, Boston: Little, Brown and Company, 1984.
Gellner, Ernest. *Nations and Nationalism*, Ithaca: Cornell University Press, 1983.
Gooch,G.P. *History and Historians in the Nineteenth Century.* Boston: Beacon Press, 1959.
Gordon, W. Terrence. *Marshall McLuhan: Escape into Understanding, a Biography,* New York: Harper Collins Publishing Inc., 1997.
Green, John Richard. *A Short History of the English People*, London: Macmillan and Co., 1881.
Hobsbawm, Eric. *On History.* New York: The New Press, 1997.
———. *Nations and Nationalism Since 1780: Programme, Myth, Reality.* New York: Cambridge University Press, 1990.
Hollis, Christopher. *The Mind of Chesterton.* London: Hollis and Carter, 1979.
———. *The Mind of Chesterton,* Coral Gables: University of Miami Press, 1970.
Huizinga, Johan. *The Waning of the Middle Ages: A Study of the Forms of Life, Thought, and Art in France and the Netherlands in the XIVth and XVth Centuries,* (New York: St. Martin's Press, 1969.
Hunter, Lynette. *G.K. Chesterton: Explorations in Allegory.* New York: St. Martin's Press, 1979.
Jaki, Stanley L. *Chesterton, A Seer of Science.* Urbana: University of Illinois Press, 1986.
Kenner, Hugh. *Paradox in Chesterton.* New York: Sheed and Ward, 1947.
Las Vernas, Raymond. *Chesterton, Belloc, Baring.* New York: Sheed & Ward, 1938.

Lauer, Quentin. G.K. *Chesterton: Philosopher Without A Portfolio.* New York: Fordham University Press, 1988.
Lea, Frank Alfred. *The Wild Knight of Battersea: G.K. Chesterton.* London: J. Clarke, 1945.
Lecky, William Edward Hartpole, *Historical and Political Essays,* New York: Longmans, Green & Co., 1908.
Mackenzie, Norman and Jeanne. *The Time Traveller: The Life of H.G. Wells.* London: Weidenfeld & Nicholson, 1973.
Mackey, Aidan. *Mr. Chesterton Comes to Tea, or How the King of England Captured Redskin Island.* Bedford, England: Vintage Publications, 1978.
McLuhan, Marshall. *The Gutenberg Galaxy: The Making of Typographic Man.* Toronto: The University of Toronto Press, 1962.
Millon-Delsol, Chantal. *L'Etat Subsidiare.* Paris: Presses Universitaires de France, 1992.
O'Connor, John. *Fr. Brown on Chesterton.* London: Oates and Washbourne, 1938.
Ong, Walter J. *Orality and Literacy.* London: Methuen & Co. Ltd., 1982.
Pearce, Joseph. *Wisdom and Innocence: A Life of G.K. Chesterton.* San Francisco: Ignatius Press, 1996.
Pieper, Josef. *In Tune With The World: A Theory of Festivity,* Chicago: Franciscan Herald Press, 1973.
Scott, Christina. *A Historian and His World: A Life of Christopher Dawson 1889–1970,* London: Sheed & Ward, 1984.
Scott, William T. *Chesterton and Other Essays* Cincinnati: Jennings and Graham, 1912.
Speaight, Robert. *The Life of Hilaire Belloc.* New York: Farrar, Straus & Cudahy, 1957.
Stannard, *Evelyn Waugh: The Early Years 1903–1939,* London: J.M. Dent and Sons, Ltd., 1986.
Sullivan, John. *G. K. Chesterton, A Centenary Appraisal.* London: Paul Elek, 1974.
———. *Chesterton Continued: A Bibliographical Supplement.* London: University of London Press, 1968.
———. *G.K. Chesterton: A Bibliography.* London: University of London Press, 1958.
———.ed. *G.K. Chesterton: A Centenary Appraisal.* London: Paul Elek, 1974.
Titterton, W.R. *G.K. Chesterton: A Portrait.* London: Douglas Organ, 1947.
Ward, Maisie. *Return to Chesterton.* New York: Sheed and Ward, 1952.
———. *Gilbert Keith Chesterton.* London: Sheed and Ward, 1944.
Waugh, Evelyn. *Brideshead Revisited,* Boston: Little, Brown and company, 1945.
———. *Edmund Campion,* New York: Sheed & Ward, 1935.
Wells, H.G. *The Outline of History.* New York: Doubleday, 1920.
West, Julius. *G.K. Chesterton: A Critical Study.* Norwood, Pennsylvania: Norwood Editions, 1978. (reprint of the 1915 ed. published by M.Secker, London).
White, Hayden. *Tropics of Discourse.* Baltimore: Johns Hopkins UP, 1978.
Wills, Garry. *Chesterton: Man and Mask.* New York: Sheed and Ward, 1961.
Zillman, Lawrence John. *The Art and Craft of Poetry,* New York: Collier Books, 1967.

SECONDARY SOURCES: PERIODICALS

Haskell, Thomas L. "Objectivity is Not Neutrality, Rhetoric vs. Practice in Peter Novick's That Noble Dream," *History and Theory* 29 (1990).

McCullagh, C. Behan. "The Truth of Historical Narratives," *History and Theory* 26.4 (1987).
Monod, Sylvere. "The Uses and Varieties of Imagination in G.K. Chesterton's *The Everlasting Man*," *The Chesterton Review* 13.1 (1987).
O'Donoghue, Noel. "Chesterton and the Philosophical Imagination," *The Chesterton Review* 24.1–2 (1998).

Index

A
Acton, Lord, 47–48
Alarms and Discursions, 20
Alfred, King, 97–103, 111, 120–121
Appetite of Tyranny, The, 11
Appreciations and Criticisms of the Works of Charles Dickens, 80
Aristotle, 13, 41, 72, 75
As I Was Saying, 4
Autobiography of G.K. Chesterton, The, 11, 75

B
Ball and the Cross, The, 2, 83, 85–91, 123, 134, 138
ballad, 97, 133
Ballad of the White Horse, The, 2, 8, 12, 18, 20, 28, 43, 83, 97–103, 107, 119–120, 132–133
Barbarism of Berlin, The, 43
Barker, Dudley, 21–22
Belloc, Hilaire, 35–37, 56, 117, 133
Boyd, Ian, 6, 20
Bloom, Harold, 34–35, 56
Brideshead Revisited, 124–125
Buckle, Henry Thomas, 44–45
Bullett, Gerald, 49–50

C
Campion, Edmund, 122–123
Canterbury Tales, The, 58
Cervantes, 109
Charles IX, 105
Charles Dickens, The Last of the Great Men, 77, 81
Chaucer, Geoffrey, 57–61, 65–67, 81–82, 122, 136–138
Cobbett, William, 51–53, 56, 71, 136–137
contract, Victorian, 69
Common Man, The, 4

Coren, Michael, 11
Corrin, Jay P., 23

D
Dale, Alzina Stone, 26–27
Dawson, Christopher, 44, 116–121
democracy, 78, 88
determinism, historical, 104
Dickens, Charles, 71, 74–82, 137–138
Distributism, 17, 23–4
Don John of Austria, 104, 111

E
Elizabeth I, 105
Everlasting Man, The, 2, 7–8, 16, 35, 39, 84–85, 92, 122
essentialism, 43
Eugenics and Other Evils, 63

F
feminism, 19
Ffinch, Michael, 18–19
Froude, J.A., 47–8

G
Gellner, Ernest, 9–10
"great man" theory of history, 7
Green, J.R., 46–47
Gooch, G.P., 46–47

H
Handful of Authors, A, 74, 133
Heretics, 3, 38
Hobsbawm, Eric, 7, 8
Hollis, Christopher, 24
humor, 3, 6, 18, 85, 93–94, 135, 138

I
imperialism, 10, 11, 25, 44, 70
Ivanhoe, 134

J
Jefferson, Thomas, 137

K
Khayyam, Omar, 23
Kipling, Rudyard, 16
Kenner, Hugh, 12–13

L
Lecky, W.E.H., 45–6
Las Vergnas, Raymond, 37
Lauer, Quentin, 14–15
locality, 1, 3, 5, 21, 33, 40, 51, 62, 78, 88, 94–96, 103, 115, 118, 135
Loved One, The, 122
Lepanto, 2, 20, 103–109, 132
Lunacy and Letters, 57, 58, 68,

M
Macaulay, Thomas, 73
Making of Europe, The, 117–120
Man Who Was Thursday, The, 2, 13, 22, 110–115, 125, 134–135
McCullagh, C. Behan, 131
McLuhan, Marshall, 116, 126–129, 136
Miller, Perry, 44
Millon-Delsol, Chantal, 30–33, 53, 102, 137

N
Napoleon of Notting Hill, The, 2, 22, 83–84, 91–97, 102, 134–135
nationalism, 1, 10, 39, 90, 118, 135
Newman, 44, 71
New Jerusalem, The, 10
novel, the, 85, 110

O
oath, medieval idea of, 69
O'Connor, Flannery, 84
Ockham, William of, 39
O'Donoghue, Noel, 57
Ong, Walter J., 107
Orthodoxy, 18, 39, 110
Outline of History, The, 39

P
patriotism, 1, 4, 10, 11, 25, 39, 41, 51, 56, 62, 75, 79, 90, 95, 103, 118, 123, 129

Pearce, Joseph, 25–26
Philip of Spain, 108
Pieper, Josef, 62
Pius V, Pope, 104
Poland, 12

R
realpolitik, 8
Richards, I.A., 127
Romance of Rhyme, The, 107

S
Scott, William, 16–17
Scott, Sir Walter, 35, 53–56, 134
Shaw, George Bernard, 3, 41–42, 56, 85
Short History of England, A, 2, 61–62, 90, 120–121
Stubbs, William, 119
subsidiarity, 30–33
Sultan of Byzantium, 104
Superstition of Divorce, The, 69,

T
Thomas, St., 39
Thomism, 15, 65,
Titterton, W.R., 17–18

U
Uses of Diverstiy, The, 82

V
Victorian Age in Literature, The, 63, 68, 71, 74
Virgil, 119
Virgin Mary, 97–98, 103
vows, societies built on, 70

W
Ward, Maisie, 25
Waugh, Evelyn, 116, 121–126
Wells, H.G., 22, 38–39, 44, 50–51, 56, 134
What's Wrong With the World, 19, 64, 126
Whig theory of history, 21–22, 24, 38, 61, 67
White, Hayden, 130
white horse, 103
Wills, Gary, 27–30
World War I, 108